SYNOPSIS OF S(

AUTHOR'S NOTE

With grateful acknowledgements to Jude Kelly and the cast of the first version, Susie Baxter, Thomas Henty, Alan Cowan, Rosalind Adler, Ben Onwukwe, and Kate Burnett, designer.

Slides of newspaper headlines and photographs are shown between the scenes. A list of these is given at the end of the script.

This play is dedicated to the memory of Thomas Henty.

Scene 1

Slide sequence. The sounds of a northern town in 1935: a busker performs to a cinema queue, a train rushes over a viaduct, a tram rattles by. A clock ticks in a back-to-back. Pause

The Lights come up on Ezra and the parrot

Ezra (*reading a newspaper*) "Do women want careers or husbands?"
Parrot Bugger off!
Ezra Ee! Our parrot! What a disappointment tha's been. It's norasif tha didn't cost money. Our Ada's spent long hours rehearsing thee, and all tha ever says is "Bugger off!" Tha's been a bad buy. All t'same, parrot, couldn't tha purra bit of effort in, today of all days?

The parrot is indifferent. Pause. The clock ticks and Ezra reads again. A woman screams in labour, off. Ezra buries himself in the "Sheffield Telegraph"

"Venizelos flees to Italian island. Greek rebel fleet surrenders."

After a moment Ezra discards the paper and turns on the wireless. Pause while it warms up

Cousin Hilda enters, stern and puritanical, but with a warm heart, if anyone could get to it

An old-fashioned BBC male newsreader's voice emerges from the radio

Radio This is the nine o'clock news from the BBC——

Cousin Hilda turns off the wireless and sniffs, which she does often

Hilda I've said it before and I'll say it again, tha'll wear out workings inside. Once a day and it'd last a lifetime.
Ezra The Duke of Norfolk's shot a rhino.
Hilda Oh ay, I hope His Highness enjoyed it. Ezra, is tha bothered mebbe about owt under this roof or am I a Chinaman?

A slight pause

She's started. Ezra? Ada's started.
Ezra Ay, I heard.

A slight pause

Hilda Has tha clapt eyes on Norah in t'last few minutes?
Ezra Out back.
Hilda Ee, deserting her post. That lass needs her mam at a time like this. She should be ashamed of herself.

Ezra In t'privy.

Hilda sniffs

Hilda Any road, Ada's doing just fine, so tha needn't worry.
Parrot Bugger off!
Hilda Ooh. I don't blame parrot. It doesn't know owt different. I blame
  Henderson. That sort of thing comes from t'top. Look at Germany. Pet
  shop? Sodom and Gommorrah more like. Every animal from that shop's
  the same—foul-mouthed.
Ezra They can't all talk. Fair do's, our Hilda. Tha's not suggesting Archie
  Halliday's goldfish swears, is tha?
Hilda It would if it could. Have you seen the look in its eye? Foul-mouthed.
  I don't know why you didn't complain. Your Ada spent good money on
  that parrot, guaranteed to be an expert in the Yorkshire dialect, and what
  does she get?
Parrot Bugger off!
Hilda Exactly. That's modern shops for you. Craftsmanship? They don't
  know the meaning of the word.

Ada screams, off

  Cousin Hilda exits

The clock ticks

Ezra (*reading*) "In your garden . . ." Come on Ada. Get it over with.

Another scream off. More reading

  "Begonias must not be over-watered."

Ada screams again

  Oh Lord, couldn't tha have thought of a better way to bring people into
  t'world?
Parrot Where there's muck there's brass.
Ezra Ee! Our parrot! Wait till our Ada hears! That's grand, that really is.
  (*He consults the paper. Then*) Thirteenth o'March, nineteen thirty-five,
  our parrot said summat besides "Bugger off"! Been hiding thy light under
  a bushel, has tha?

  *Her Mother enters, nearly seventy, forthright, long-suffering and pessimis-
  tic*

  Ee, Norah, tha'll never believe . . .
Norah I know I wouldn't mesen if I hadn't seen it with me own eyes and
  nose. Her next-door hasn't scoured it out or nowt.

*A slight pause. Ezra thinks better of it and buries himself in the "Sheffield
Telegraph" again*

  Sharing a lavie means sharing the cleaning.

Ada screams, off

It's a right difficult one.

Ezra Hitler has announced air parity with Britain.

A slight pause. Norah looks at Ezra

Norah I said it's a right difficult one. Our first allus are on our side. I had devil's own job with Ada hersen'.

A slight pause. Norah looks at him again

We haven't heard owt from our Doris, then?

Ezra Happen she's occupied.

Norah Humph!

Ezra Happen there's a crisis. Her Teddy's got important business interests, which can never take second place.

Norah Her Teddy! Ashamed of her own flesh and blood more like . . . But I'm saying nowt.

Ezra (*reading*) "Headless corpse found in canal; is it missing Thurmarsh newsagent?"

Norah It's nearly Thursday already, it wouldn't surprise me if it's not born while Friday.

Ezra Tha doesn't mean Cousin Hilda'll be staying the night, does tha?

Norah Ezra Pratt! Eee, what I could say but I won't.

A slight pause

How many pocket knives did tha' manage this week then?

Ezra Penknives, Norah, I make penknives. I'm a two-ended man. I wouldn't lower mesen' to make pocket knives.

Norah Humph! Tha wouldn't catch Cousin Hilda's gentlemen lodgers lowerin' theysen to make knives. Or forks.

Ezra I'm not risin' to t'bait, I won't gi' thee satisfaction.

A slight pause

Norah Ee, our Doris should be here.

Ada screams again, off. Norah goes to exit. Henry gives a long, wailing, baby's cry, off stage

Ezra Eh, Norah! Not born while Friday, did tha say?

Norah I never! I knew it'd not keep us hanging about. She's plenty big enough, after all.

Norah exits

Ezra Hey up, our parrot! I'm a father!

Parrot Bugger off!

Ezra exits

Music. Lights fade slightly. Noise of Ezra, Ada, Cousin Hilda and Norah sleeping. The parrot puts a cloth over itself. Pause. The parrot screams under the cloth

Ezra enters

Ezra Ee, our Ada's having another baby!

The parrot screams again. Ezra removes the cloth, cutting short the scream. They look at each other. It screams again. Then

Taking mickey out of a woman in childbirth, is tha?! I love thee, Ada. No creature has the right to mock thy suffering ... and live!

Ezra strangles the parrot which protests. Then to himself, the parrot dead

Ada, I killed parrot for love of thee, my darling.
Ada (*off*) Ezra, is summat up wi' me parrot!
Ezra (*calling*) I had a do it in, Ada.
Ada (*off*) Aagh!
Ezra (*calling*) It were a dead loss! All it ever said were, "Bugger off!"

The parrot revives for a last dying gasp

Parrot There's nowt so queer as folk.

The parrot dies finally. Music: "There'll Always Be an England". Slide sequence. 1935 to 1938

SCENE 2

The Lights come up on the Radio, Henry and Ezra

Radio Fleetwood-Smith to bowl to Hutton. The tension's mounting here at the Oval. Len Hutton's score stands at three hundred and thirty-two. He needs just three runs to beat the record of three hundred and thirty-four held by Don Bradman. It's jolly exciting. Fleetwood-Smith bowls. He drops it short. Hutton cuts.

During the above ...

Henry Look, Dad, I deaded an inseck. Look.
Ezra Ay, lad, shut up now.
Henry Dad, I deaded him a lot, look.
Ezra Grand, boy, shut up a minute.

Henry squashes the insect on the floor

Henry He's all squashed now, Dad, look.
Ezra Sod off, will you!

A loud cheer from the wireless. Henry screams and yells

Ada and Norah enter. Ada is in her thirties, plain and ordinary and proud of it, more assertive than Ezra but just as vulnerable deep down

"For He's a Jolly Good Fellow" plays on the wireless

Ada Let's get this right, tha told our little Henry to sod off because of cricket?

Ezra Ay, Ada, but Len Hutton were making highest test score ever. It were the greatest moment in English cricket history, ruined.

Ada Good.

Norah I'm saying nowt.

Ada Shut up, Mother.

Norah I haven't said owt.

Ada And that's enough from you, Henry.

Ezra Ay, teach little porker to keep his gob shut.

Ada Don't you call our Henry, "little porker".

Norah Tha's norra fatty, is tha, Henry? He'll grow out of t'podgy stage.

Ada Shut up, Mother. (*To Ezra*) You'll just have to make it up to him now.

Music. Slide sequence

SCENE 3

The Lights come up on Ezra and Henry

Tram ride, bus ride, sounds of town merging into country

Ezra Did you enjoy the bus ride, our Henry?

Henry Ay, Dad.

Ezra Sheffield and Peak District, a mucky picture set in a golden frame. Right then, picnic. We've got us brawn to contend with. I hate brawn. I hate gravy too. I like me food dry. It's more than my life's worth to tell Ada that. In life, Henry, tha has to eat a lot gravy tha doesn't want. There's going to be a war. That's what Reg Hammond reckons any road. The world is changing. Think on, though, our Henry, before tha blames us for bringing thee into t'world. Remember this. Tha's English. Tha's Yorkshire. Tha could have been born Nepalese or Belgian or in Surrey or owt. Thank me for that, at least.

Henry Ay, Dad.

Ezra It's not going to be easy, lad.

Henry Isn't it, Dad?

Ezra No, Henry, it isn't, but tha'll shape up. Thy little mind's never still. Tha's got brains. Brains and brawn. Tha'll do. Tha'll do.

Henry (*screaming*) Aagh! (*He clings to his father*)

Ezra Hell's bells! We've come for a picnic. We've come for us treat.

Henry Don't leave me here! Don't go home wi' out me! Aagh! Don't tell me to sod off again!

Ezra What's tha on about? Nay, lad, tha's not nesh, is tha? We don't want kids at school calling us nesh, do we?

Henry Aagh!

Ezra Oh heck.

A radio comedy programme is heard. Slide sequence. 1938 to 1939 and September 1939

SCENE 4

The Lights come up on Ada, Ezra and Norah

Ada Look at him. Is he fighting material? If Hitler's crack Panzer divisions see a scranny feller like him coming towards them will they panic?

Ezra I'll be serving my country. Think on, Ada, what would tha reckon to me if I let others do all t'fighting?

Ada There's ways to serve thy country baht volunteering.

Norah Ay, I thought tha liked being an air-raid warden?

Ada Ay, tha looks just grand wi' t'helmet and navy blue pullover wi' yellow stripes.

Norah Navy blue suits him. I've allus said that.

Ezra I'm talking about resisting evil demands of t'fascist dictator not navy blue pullovers wi' yellow stripes.

Norah I'm saying nowt.

Ezra Any road, it's too late now. I'm off tomorrow.

Ada I know.

Ezra It's me last night.

Norah (*yawning meaningfully*) I think mebbe I'll just go and get ready for bed.

Ada It's only eight o'clock.

Norah Ay, but ... I'm feeling a little sleepy. (*Yawning*) You know. So, I think I will go on up. I expect I'll be asleep as soon as my head hits the pillow.

Norah exits

Ezra Ada?

Ada (*with some dread*) What?

Ezra About Henry.

Ada Wharra 'bout him?

Ezra Take him to Kate's. Get him away from here.

Ada Become evacuees, does tha mean?

Ezra Not evacuees. It's not evacuees, isn't staying wi' relations. While I'm in front line, fighting Jerry, I want to know our kid's safe.

Ada We won't be any safer up there if there's an invasion.

Ezra Course you will. Any road, there won't be an invasion. There'll be bombing, though.

Ada They won't bomb civilians.

Ezra We won't. We've said we won't. They will. They're ruthless killers. Go, Ada. It's best.

Pause

  Ada?

Ada I've gorra headache.

Ezra It's me last night. I might never come back.

Ada Oh, Ezra, don't say that.

Ezra It's a possibility, Ada. It's got to be faced.

Ada I'm not making excuses, Ezra, I have gorra headache.
Ezra Is it bad headache?
Ada Oh, you go on up. I'll just make t'door.

Music. Slide. The sound of ancient bed-springs

Ezra Ooh, Ada. Is tha warm enough?
Ada Aagh! Ezra, watch tha elbow, will tha?
Ezra Ee, Ada, tha's beautiful, tha's picture of Veronica Lake.
Ada Gerraway wi' yer. Oh. Ah.

More bed-springs

   Henry enters

Henry Stop it! Stop it, Dad! Give over! What's tha doing under them covers? Tha's hurting her! Don't do that to me mam!
Ezra Oh hell's bells, our Henry, hell's bells!

Music. Slide sequence. September, 1939

SCENE 5

The Lights come up on Ada and Henry

Ada They said they'd be here early doors. Some folk have a queer idea of early doors. Still it's nice of Uncle Teddy and Aunty Doris to take us to Kate's, isn't it, Henry?
Henry I hate Kate.
Ada Shut up, Henry.

Aunty Doris and Uncle Teddy enter, two social climbers, roped together climbing up towards the nouveau riche. She in the newest clothes, strong perfume and dyed hair, he bluff and a little shifty. They are about forty in nineteen forty

Doris Ooh, is that Henry? Podgy little chap, isn't he, Teddy?
Ada He'll grow out of it. Cup of tea?
Teddy No, we're all right, thanks. We've got a long way to go and there's the black-out.
Doris I know our Leonard's got more room but I do wish Mother had asked to come to us. We'd have been happy to have her, wouldn't we, Teddy?
Teddy (*meaning the luggage*) Is this all there is?
Doris Teddy!
Teddy Well, there's not much, to say they're going for t'duration.
Doris (*hissing*) Tact!
Teddy What the hell d'you mean, tact?
Doris I mean don't rub it in that some folk haven't got as much as others.

Teddy Oh ay, right. (*Quietly to Doris*) You've made things worse by protesting about it, Doris.

Doris (*publicly*) It's rude to whisper, Teddy love.

Teddy (*to Ada*) Travelling light, eh? That's the ticket. Soon get this lot into the boot, the rest of your stuff'll be safe here.

Doris (*to Henry*) Your Uncle Teddy's got a new car, Henry. It's an Armstrong-Siddeley twelve-plus saloon de-luxe.

Henry I don't want to go.

Ada It's nice there, Henry.

Teddy Now you've not forgotten anything? Because I'm not turning back.

Doris He never turns back.

Ada I've not forgotten owt.

Teddy I've got the brown paper bag. In case he's car-sick.

Doris Teddy! You didn't have to say what it's for. It's obvious. You could have just handed it to her later. You've made things worse.

Teddy You've made things worse by protesting about it.

Doris Teddy, you've just put the idea of being sick into his head, that's all.

Teddy You won't be sick, will you, Henry?

Henry No, Uncle Teddy. (*Henry smiles privately*)

Ada Let's gerron wi' it.

Doris He has to have his little argument.

Teddy (*through clenched teeth*) I do not have to have my little argument. I do not have to have my little argument, Doris.

Doris Don't clench your teeth at me.

Teddy Can we go now? I mean, who are we supposed to be fighting, Germans, or ourselves.

Ada (*half to herself*) Nobody, in your case.

Doris and Teddy freeze

Teddy I have flat feet. I have very flat feet. I have fallen arches. My worst enemy couldn't say that I am a man not to face the music when the chips are down. I want to do my bit, but with my feet I've no chance. No chance.

Ada I'm sorry.

Teddy That's all right. We'll attribute it to tension and wipe it from the minutes.

Doris I've forgotten it completely already, Ada, dear.

Teddy Shut t'door then. Who knows, maybe for the last time.

Doris (*hissing*) Teddy! We are perfectly well aware, thank you very much, that Ada's house is a prime bomb target.

Teddy Doris!

Doris That is my name Teddy. Please stop pulling faces. (*To Henry*) I'm your mummy's sister, Henry.

Ada Older.

Doris Lovely Low Farm at Rowth Bridge. Lovely Aunty Kate and Uncle Frank.

Teddy Don't expect you'll enjoy countryside a lot, eh Ada? Devastated, I shouldn't wonder, worrying about what's happening to your Ezra.

Doris Teddy! Ada doesn't need you to draw attention to the terrible mortal danger her husband is in. Hourly.

Despairing gesture from Teddy. Then Doris continues to Henry

You'll have to take care of your mummy now, won't you, Henry?

Henry kisses his mother's hand

Ah!
Teddy For crying out loud, look, can we get in t'car before I'm the one who's sick.

Music. Slide sequence

SCENE 6

Sounds of the countryside in winter, sheep to the fore

Henry is hand-in-hand with Billy The Half-Wit, a slow, nice, retarded countryman

Henry What did sheepdog get for Christmas, Billy?
Billy Don't be daft. Tha doesn't gi' dog presents.
Henry Aunty Kate told me tha weren't all there.
Billy Tha's right. But I work hard. And folks can't be choosy with a war on. Frank Turnbull's been good to me.
Henry Where's the rest of thee?

Pause

Billy Tha' mother's a town biddy. Frank Turnbull said.
Henry Is Uncle Frank your Uncle Frank?
Billy Don't be daft. Can tha believe, not even coming wi' a pair of wellies.
Henry We didn't know about muck. T'other hand is right warm now, in me pocket, Billy.
Billy I'm looking after you. I'm watching sheep.
Henry I'm watching snow. Won't they die?
Billy Grown-up sheep are very tough. It's when we get snow in lambing season that we're in trouble.
Henry This is my best home ever.
Billy This isn't thy home, Henry. I know. It can be right cruel and lonely. Thy mother cries when tha's not looking.
Henry Does she Billy?
Billy Thy Uncle Frank said. She thinks tha don't love her no more. She thinks tha loves new-fangled places, new friends and new relatives more than thy old mam.
Henry (*happily*) Ay, I do.
Billy Tha should try not to. Thy mam's got a man at war.
Henry Oh I can't, Billy. This place is better than loving me mam! Any road, she shouldn't cry. I didn't cry when I ate Christmas goose. I were right put

out at first, 'cos I knew 'im. He were my friend. But I ate him, and he were right tasty and all.

A slight pause

Them in t'house were on about me startin' school, Billy. I'm not keen mesen, I said I'm not struck, Billy.

Billy What's tha gonna do when tha's growed? Tha's got to do tha' lessons.

Henry I want to grow up like you, Billy. I want to be a half-wit and work wi' you on t' farm.

Music. Slide sequence, 1940

SCENE 7

Comic cut-outs. Henry reads the "Beano" in a barn

Eric Lugg enters, an almost grown-up lad from a family of trouble-makers. Eric carries a venomous looking hoe

Eric What's tha doing in this barn?

Henry Oh cripes! It's Eric Lugg! Look at that hoe!

Eric Ay, lad, mark it well. Eric Lugg I be. And tha's trespassing, squirt.

Henry This barn belongs to Lorna Arrow's dad. She said I could be here. I'm waiting for her.

Eric Hang on, I know thee. You're that cissy squirt evacuee from up at Turnbulls.

Henry I'm not an evacuee. I'm staying wi' relations. I'm not afraid of thee, tha don't own this barn, you Luggs don't own anything, apart from a rat-infested cottage and a back garden full of rusty bikes and sundry bric-a-brac.

Eric I'm a terror round these parts, does tha know that, pansy?

Henry Me Uncle Frank and me Aunty Kate say that you Luggs should be put a stop to. They reckon you're a blemish on the face of Rowth Bridge village.

Eric I'll kill thee!

Henry No tha won't.

Eric I'll skewer thee wi' me hoe!

Henry Tha wouldn't dare.

Eric I'll stand next to thee and give thee nits.

Henry Don't tha come near me.

Eric Tha's teacher's pet, in't tha?

Henry Miss Candy is interested in my progress, that's all. She doesn't believe in favouritism.

Eric Has tha seen her titties?

Henry (*squealing with shock*) Eeooaagh!

Eric We all know she has moustache, 'cos we can see it, and that she's as fat as a pregnant cow, but does tha know she's got great tufts of hair all over?

Henry Tha's making it up. How does tha know?

Eric She used to be a stripper in a club.
Henry Where?
Eric Wakefield.
Henry I don't believe it.
Eric And she keeps a giant seal in her bath.
Henry What for?
Eric She used to train 'em in t'circus. And she swigs a bottle of gin a day. And she was loved by a Yank who ran off and left her. Who'd blame him? But does tha know what she does to her favourite cissy teacher's pet after about a month or two?
Henry What, Eric, what does she do?
Eric Er ... Tha'll find out. Now clear out.

Lorna Arrow enters, a girl the same age as Henry, flighty and excitable, already a natural flirt

Lorna Oh, it's horrid, smelly Eric Lugg. What on earth are you doing in my dad's barn?
Eric Just inspecting it, Miss Arrow.
Henry Hallo, Lorna.
Lorna (*to Eric*) Does tha take me for an infant? I am eight. You are backsliding and trying to get out of work. What was he saying to you, Henry?
Henry He was just saying funny things about Miss Candy.
Lorna Oh you disgusting beast! Spreading those vile rumours. I wouldn't be surprised if only half of them are totally true. Miss Candy is just a poor, maligned spinster school-teacher of fifty-three who's hideously ugly. Was he frightening you, Henry? I bet he was.
Henry (*doubtfully*) No.
Eric Cissy'd be frightened of a runt piglet.
Lorna Leave this barn on the instant, or I shall report you to my dad, and then that will be the end of casual employment on the Arrows' farm for you!
Eric All right, I'm going. (*Threatening them*) But I'm not running away. Some of us have got to bale hay. (*To Henry*) Eh, lad, keep thy hand on tha sixpence, she'll violate thy purity given half a chance. Ha, ha, ha.

Eric Lugg exits, laughing

Lorna Hallo. Which does tha prefer, Henry, greengages or eggs?
Henry Both.
Lorna Tha can have a greengage for tha breakfast then. Ha, ha. (*Then, suggestively*) Come and sit down next to me and read comics to me.
Henry Me mood isn't right. Does tha think I'm advanced for me years?
Lorna (*suggestively again*) Ay, I do. I think tha's right good at tha lessons too. No, really!
Henry (*mystified by her strange tone*) That's all right, I know I am.
Lorna Conceitedness is not at all a nice thing in a boy. Any road ... (*she chants*) ... you're a fat useless lump, that's what everybody says.
Henry I aren't. I'll show you.

Lorna Oh do, do, do!

Henry Don't want to.

Lorna Who was the only person not to laugh at you on sports day?

Henry I didn't come last in everything.

Lorna No, not the sack race, but I think you are forgetting the hundred
yards, the four forty, the egg and spoon race, the high jump, the three-
legged race and potato race. Last every time is quite a record.

*Pause. Lorna suddenly lifts her skirt, showing him her knickers briefly. Henry
blinks in confusion and disbelief*

Any road, it's the holidays now. Yippee!

*Lorna chases Henry. He tries to avoid her and do something safer, like reading
his comic*

Henry I'll read to thee. Lord Snooty and his pals . . .

Lorna I'm bored with that. Which would tha prefer, Henry, a castle with six
gold doors or sixteen tons of "All Bran"?

Henry Which would tha prefer, a smack in the gob or a kick up t'arse end?

Lorna exits screaming tearfully

Slide sequence

SCENE 8

Sounds of a third division football match followed by that of a train journey

Miss Candy is escorting young Henry. Miss Candy has a far-back voice

Miss Candy Well, Henry, and what did you think of the game?

Henry It were the greatest football match in the world, miss.

Miss Candy Wasn't it just, Henry?! And are you enjoying the train ride?

Henry Oh, ay, miss.

Miss Candy There's no better team on God's earth than Bradford City,
even in the Wartime League North.

Henry In the first half I supported Leeds and they scored two goals, and
second half I supported Bradford and they scored two goals, so I was
supporting winning side throughout t'match. That was good, wasn't it,
miss?

Miss Candy That was very good, Henry.

Henry (*in wonderment*) Are they really greatest team on God's earth, are
they, miss?

Miss Candy No, I'm sorry, Henry, not really, but it's great fun to think so.
Getting all excited and worked up! Shouting at the ref, "Other way, ref!
Where's your white stick, you fool!" It's so exhilarating.

Henry Miss Candy?

Miss Candy Yes, Henry.

Henry Me dad's coming home on leave soon. He's been wounded. In his eye. Me mam's going to Portsmouth to meet him. Miss Candy?
Miss Candy Yes, Henry.
Henry I want to stay at your school. I don't ever want to leave Low Farm, ever.
Miss Candy You'll have to go back to your own home when the war's over.
Henry You know, I were right bothered at match when tha were shouting and everything. All the men were looking at you.
Miss Candy Yes, but they tend to do that anyway.
Henry I don't think tha needs a shave, Miss Candy.

A slight pause

Miss Candy That's very kind of you. Henry, since you have had such an enjoyable day, I want you to do something for me. I know people say certain things about me. I want you to tell me what they say, Henry. It'll be good for me.
Henry Everything?
Miss Candy Oh yes, absolutely everything.

Pause

Henry Oh double heck.

Music. Slide sequence. 1940 to 1945

SCENE 9

The Lights come up on Miss Forest, headmistress, in her room. Miss Forest is a brisk, no-nonsense, self-confident and self-righteous headmistress

Miss Candy enters in high dudgeon

Miss Candy Miss Forest.
Miss Forest Miss Candy.
Miss Candy Just now . . .
Miss Forest Yes.
Miss Candy Miss Forest, just now without so much as a by-your-leave the Pratt boy was whisked out of my classroom . . .
Miss Forest By me.
Miss Candy By you. And if I may say so in a most imperious manner.
Miss Forest I am sorry that you feel belittled by my actions, Miss Candy . . .
Miss Candy I didn't say that.
Miss Forest May I be clear what is required?
Miss Candy I wish you to knock on my classroom door before entering in future.
Miss Forest You do?
Miss Candy I do.
Miss Forest At all times, Miss Candy?
Miss Candy It seems reasonable, Miss Forest.

Miss Forest I take it you wouldn't object if I were to omit the knock in the case of a fire for example?

Miss Candy Obviously not in the case of a fire.

Miss Forest Or in the case of an act of God, Miss Candy?

Miss Candy In the case of an act of God, yes, you may omit the knock, Miss Forest.

Miss Forest Thank you. How about in the case of the Pratt boy's mother being run over by a bus?

A slight pause

Miss Candy Has the Pratt boy's mother been run over by a bus?

Miss Forest (*smiling at Miss Candy*) Yes, Miss Candy, isn't it terrible? The driver stood no chance. It happened in Portsmouth. Ada Pratt had apparently gone there to greet her husband. She was crossing the road, about to embrace him, I believe. Tragic, under the circumstances, I'm sure you'll agree, Miss Candy?

Miss Candy I'm sorry, I . . .

Miss Forest I accept your apology.

Pause

Miss Candy Miss Forest . . . ?

Miss Forest Naturally the boy will be returning to live with his father in Thurmarsh. Now if you will excuse me . . .

Miss Candy Poor Henry.

Miss Forest We can't afford to be sentimental, can we? After all there is a war on, or rather, there was. A word about your teaching methods, I don't approve of favouritism, and neither do the parents. I thought I'd mention it. Good. Now, the VE Day celebrations. I trust I can leave the catering to you?

Radio comedy programmes are heard. Slide sequence

SCENE 10

The Lights come up on Mr Gibbins' classroom

Mr Gibbins is a sincere but weary teacher, weary of boys in general and these boys in particular

Henry enters

Henry Er . . . is this Form Two?

Mr Gibbins You must be the new boy. The returning evacuee.

Henry I weren't an evacuee. I were staying with relations.

Mr Gibbins Same thing.

Henry I were staying at Low Farm. It's at Rowth Bridge, Upper Mitherdale.

Mr Gibbins Oh, a geography specialist.

The boys laugh, Henry is mortified

Well, welcome back to Thurmarsh, near Sheffield. I'm Mr Gibbins. Who are you?

Henry Henry.

Mr Gibbins Henry what?

Henry Henry Pratt.

Mr Gibbins Henry Pratt what?

Henry Just Henry Pratt.

Mr Gibbins At your last school, in Rowth Bridge, Upper Mitherdale——

Sniggers from the boys

—if your teacher had said, "What is your name?" what would you have said?

Henry Ezra.

Mr Gibbins I thought you said your name was Henry.

Henry Ay, it is, but there were another Henry, and they couldn't have two Henrys so they called me Ezra in t'school.

Mr Gibbins I see. Now Pratt, when you addressed your teacher, in Rowth Bridge, Upper Mitherdale——

More sniggers

—did you use a little word as a mark of respect to that teacher?

Henry Oh ay.

Mr Gibbins Well, we believe in respect for authority here at Brunswick Road Primary, so I'd like you to use the same little word to me. Do you understand?

Henry Oh ay.

Mr Gibbins Oh ay what?

Henry Oh ay, miss.

Mr Gibbins is non-plussed. The boys collapse in laughter. Music. Change of scene. Playground noise

The Paradise Lane Gang enter

Hallo, Martin, hallo, Tommy, hallo, Basher, hallo, Slasher.

Gang Hallo, Henry.

Henry What's Paradise Lane Gang doing tonight?

The boys tap their noses and jeer

Martin We all know what you're doing? You're looking after your one-eyed dad.

Laughter

Henry Me dad lost that eye fighting Germans, Martin Hammond!

Basher I heard he'd pawned it down t'*Navigation* pub for half a pint.

Laughter

Martin (*pointing to his eye*) Ay, ay.

Laughter

Henry I'll get thee, Martin Hammond!

Henry tries to hit Martin. The boys beat Henry to the ground

Gang 'Bye, Henry.

Music. Slide sequence

SCENE 11

The Lights come up on Henry reading at home

After a pause, Cousin Hilda enters

Hilda Where's our Ezra? He's never gone down t'pub and left you on your own, 'as he?

Henry No, Cousin Hilda. He's gone for a walk. He likes walking.

Hilda Does he often go out and leave you on your own?

A slight pause

Henry It's right nice of thee to come and see us unexpected like, Cousin Hilda.

Hilda Does tha dad often go out and leave you on your own?

Henry He might pop down t'*Navigation* for a quick bevvy now and then. But not often.

Hilda Does he treat you all right?

Henry Course he does, he's me dad!

Hilda Ay, I know. But war's a terrible thing, Henry. It upsets people's nerves. Sometimes they go a bit . . . well . . . funny. It's not their fault, so if he did go a bit . . . well . . . funny, there wouldn't be any reason not to tell anybody, would there?

Henry No, Cousin Hilda.

Hilda What's tha reading?

Henry Book.

Hilda Y' cheeky ha'porth. Lerusava look.

He hands over the book

Henry It's me favourite.

Hilda (*reading the title*) Biggles Flies North. Great one for the reading, is tha?

Henry I've read tons of books. I've read, *Biggles Flies North*, this is me second time, *Biggles Flies South*, *Biggles Flies East*, *Biggles Flies West*, *Biggles Flies In*, *Biggles Flies Out*, *Biggles Sweeps The Desert*.

Hilda Mm. Well, I'm going to set to. This place looks as though it hasn't seen a duster since VE Day.

Cousin Hilda exits

Henry ponders

Henry I'll write me own books! (*He picks up a pencil and an exercise book. He writes*) "Chapter one ..." (*A slight pause. He sucks the pencil*) A bit hard startin' straight off like. I'll write down a list of titles and then decide which one to write first. (*After a pause, he writes*)

Cousin Hilda enters

Hilda I were thinking. Is your dad happy?

Henry I don't think he likes not having a job.

Hilda Does his having one eye upset you?

Henry No, they made right good job of false one. Cousin Hilda, me and me dad're right grateful to thee for coming to do dusting, but I've got us homework to do.

Hilda Is that your homework? (*Cousin Hilda takes the book from him and reads*) "Pratt Flies North", "Pratt Flies South", "Pratt Flies East", "Pratt Flies West", "Pratt Sweeps The Desert", "What Is Happiness?"

Henry We've got to write a book. I were just listing me titles.

Hilda Nay, lad, day-dreams. They're all about you.

Henry Oh that isn't me, it's me dad.

Hilda Oh ay. Any road, you don't loop your "p"s right. I'll get on wi' cleaning.

Cousin Hilda exits

Henry (*writing*) "Squadron Leader Ezra Pratt, known to all his chums as "Prattles", stood on t'steps of Royal Aero Club ..."

Ezra enters

Cousin Hilda's upstairs.

Ezra What's she doing here?

Henry Dusting. I told her tha'd gone for a walk.

Ezra (*amazed*) Well done, lad, well done! If she thought I'd been down t'*Navigation* she'd have torn bollocks off me.

Henry It's a good job tha came back early.

Ezra Ay, well, it seems I'm not welcome at t'*Navigation* any more. He says to me tonight, tha's here all night every night. I were flambergasted. I said, "So what? Tha's open, in't tha? I'm entitled." "Tha's not entitled wi'out I say so," he says. "I'm entitled to refuse to serve anybody. Patrons don't like thee going on about t'war. War's over." "Ay, I know", I said, "because I bloody fought it. That's why it's over. Don't give me "patrons". It's thee," I said. "Tha's never liked me." That struck home 'cause he hasn't, and I'll tell thee why. 'Cause I don't like what he's done t'pub. I didn't fight Hitler for five years so he could put bright green upholstery in t'snug. "Tha's never liked me," I said. "I go away for five years, and what happens? My place in dominoes team gets taken. It's a bloody disgrace." "They couldn't play a man short for five years," he said. "Ay", I said, "fair enough, Cecil, point taken, but I'm back now. Darts, fair enough, I'm a shadow of me former self wi' one eye, but not dominoes. I played Reg Hammond last night, and I won six games end away." "Ay", he said, "but I can't split up a winning combination." Reg

Hammond, to his eternal credit, offered to stand down. I refused. "Thanks, Reg", I said, "much appreciated, but no. I don't want to be the *cause célèbre* of a domino crisis." But I never thought I'd be banned from t'pub. Sorry, lad, I didn't mean to bother thee with my problems.

Cousin Hilda enters

Hilda Oh, you're back.
Ezra I just went out for a spot of air.
Hilda Oh ay. Three times round bar of t'*Navigation*?
Ezra Just o'er t'river, just round t'roads.
Hilda This place is a pigsty. I could write me name in t'dust on your wardrobe, and the rag-rug's coming unravelled.
Ezra Oh shut up.
Hilda Well, I can't stop here all night, I've got my gentlemen lodgers to see to. (*She sniffs*) Well, don't bother, I'll show mesen out. (*She sniffs again*) Did you walk round canal, or drink it?

Cousin Hilda exits

Music. Slide sequence. 1946

SCENE 12

The Lights come up on Cousin Hilda with Liam O'Reilly, one of her gentlemen lodgers. Mr O'Reilly is pleasant, well-meaning and anxious to help, if somewhat hesitant

Hilda Mr O'Reilly, did tha enjoy tea then?
Liam Oh, yes, it was very nice, thank you, yes.
Hilda Because tha's only got to say. I can take criticism.
Liam It was very nice, yes. But since you——
Hilda Good! I've had a very trying day, Mr O'Reilly. Does tha know our Henry?
Liam Oh yes, I t'ink I met him once before . . .
Hilda No, I don't think tha did.
Liam That's right, I don't t'ink I did, no.
Hilda He's passed 'is eleven plus.
Liam Oh, that's very good, yes.
Hilda I've been out most o't'day shopping for his uniform for t'grammar school and all t'other bits and pieces. I mean, it's not my place. Has tha met his father?
Liam Oh yes, I t'ink I met him once.
Hilda No, I don't think tha did.
Liam That's right, I don't t'ink I did, no.
Hilda Does he show an interest? Too busy getting pints down him in t'pub. Mr O'Reilly, I don't know owt about boys. I don't know owt about boys or men. That's where you come in.

Alarm registers faintly on Mr O'Reilly's otherwise blank face

I've got to get it off me chest and I've decided to use you. Mr O'Reilly, can I treat you like a doctor?

A very slight pause

Liam Well, yes, if you like, yes.

Hilda Good. Mr O'Reilly, this is not going to be easy for me.

Liam (*utterly bewildered*) Oh, I see. Yes.

Hilda I am very, very, very worried. About Henry's ... is tha with me, Mr O'Reilly?

Liam Oh yes, yes, yes.

Hilda About his ... body. A particular part of his ... of his ... er ... of his little body. Er ... it's down ... down t'bottom ... and round t'back. Is tha with me, Mr O'Reilly?

Liam Well, yes, right with you, oh yes, yes.

Hilda T'other day in school, Henry er ... from the bit of the body that I've just described ... er, he made ... um, well, he couldn't help hissen. He made ... um ... tha knows tha does sometimes when tha's least expecting, and there's nothing tha can do ... a little noise.

Liam You mean he broke wind.

Hilda Mr O'Reilly!! I'm finding this very difficult as 'tis.

Liam Oh, I see, yes.

Hilda But tha's right, that is what I'm talking about. But it weren't a little 'un, by all accounts it were a right corker. T'other boys all stood up and cheered. He were offered life membership of Paradise Lane Gang on t'strength of it. Any road, it turned out lads expected him to have it on tap. And when he weren't up to t'repeat performance they were very, very angry. They threw him in t'Rundle. Which is norra nice canal. Mr O'Reilly, I had no idea. Who'd have thought ... that ... were a sign o'manliness? Come to think on it, I suppose tha can do it? If I were to say, Mr O'Reilly, prove yoursen, tha could, could tha?

Liam I wouldn't like to try at this moment. You know, I mean I have done it once or twice, in the past ... at Christmas and ... but I wouldn't like to do it right now.

Hilda And tha doesn't feel half a man or owt?

Liam I t'ink you might've got the wrong end of the stick, sort of thing.

Hilda Mr O'Reilly, tha must gi' me peace of mind. Will he be all right? Is he normal? Will he be able to have babies? I just don't know.

Liam What happened ... I t'ink ... it was a slight fluke. That's all. It was like a one-off thing, that's all. How can I put it? The little bit at the front, and the er ... bit at the back ... they aren't connected at all, in a manner of speaking. You can put your mind at rest. Oh yes.

Hilda Oh, Mr O'Reilly, would tha like some ginger beer!?

Liam Well, no, but if you've got—

Hilda I'll get tha a big glass full—

Liam Oh, yes, thank you. Let's be leaving the lad to his books. You and me, we'll drink to the biggest fart in history, aren't I right now, Hilda? (*He puts a hand on her leg*)

Hilda Mr O'Reilly!!!

Cousin Hilda is shocked beyond belief. Music: "The March of the Dambusters"

Henry rushes about playing aeroplanes

Slide sequence. 1945. The dropping of the atomic bomb

SCENE 13

The noises of a boys' grammar school

The Lights come up on Henry, who is met by Mr Quell, his form-master. Mr Quell is sincere, responsible and rather self-conscious in company. He wears an academic gown and carries a briefcase

Mr Quell Pratt, I want a word with you about your essay.
Henry Oh, do you, Mr Quell?
Mr Quell It's Henry, isn't it.
Henry Yes, sir.
Mr Quell Let's sit down.

They do

"The Best Day of my Holidays." So many boys chose Christmas, you strove for more originality than that.
Henry I didn't have a very good Christmas, Mr Quell.
Mr Quell The day you've chosen begins badly. You haven't slept well. Your father has had nightmares. You're tired. So how is this to be "The Best Day of my Holidays"? I am intrigued. I read on out of curiosity not duty. This is rare, Henry. Particularly for a boy in the first year.
Henry Thank you, sir.
Mr Quell You seem to spend a great deal of the day reading.
Henry I like reading, sir.
Mr Quell Good. Who are your favourite authors?
Henry Oh, Captain W. E. Johns is the greatest author that ever lived. I've read all the "Biggles", books and I've got his Gimlet books from the library now.
Mr Quell "Gimlet"?
Henry They're almost as good as, "Biggles". There's, *Gimlet Flies East, Gimlet Flies West, Gimlet Flies South, Gimlet Flies North.* I once got out a book called, *Hamlet,* sir. I thought it was *Gimlet.* It was rubbish.
Mr Quell Shall we get back to your essay? You read for three hours, pausing only to say, "Oh, goodbye". That is to your father.
Henry Yes, sir.
Mr Quell Where was he going?
Henry Don't know sir.
Mr Quell The pub?
Henry Don't know, sir.
Mr Quell All right. You return to your book, and then you get the dinner. Your father comes back?

Henry Yes, sir.
Mr Quell More reading ensues. You get the tea. You wash up. What about your father?
Henry His nerves are bad, and he's been a bit worse since he lost the new job Uncle Teddy'd given him. So it's best if I do it, sir.
Mr Quell You bury yourself in a book yet again. You go to bed. You hear your father come in. From this we may safely deduce that he'd gone out again?
Henry Yes, sir.
Mr Quell Where to?
Henry Don't know, sir.
Mr Quell The pub?
Henry Don't know, sir.
Mr Quell You lie in bed and you hear your father come up the stairs. He comes into your room and tells you that he's been fighting a villainous plot to overthrow the government and kill the king. And then your adventure begins. You go out with your father and help him save the nation and bring the villainous thugs to heel.
Henry Yes, sir.
Mr Quell This dream, this fantasy, in which your father is a hero, this is what makes this, "The Best Day of the Holidays"?
Henry Yes, sir.
Mr Quell It's imaginative. It's different. It's good. You mentioned an uncle, do you have any other relatives?
Henry Ay, Mr Quell. There's Uncle Teddy, like I said, and Aunty Doris . . . and Cousin Hilda.
Mr Quell Will you tell me where they live?

Radio comedy programme. Slide sequence

SCENE 14

The Lights come up on Henry's house

Henry is listening to the radio. Uncle Teddy, Aunty Doris, Cousin Hilda and Mr Quell, in overcoat but with his briefcase, are looking for Ezra

Hilda Henry, that wireless'll be wore out then tha'll be sorry. (*She switches off the radio*)
Doris This room, it's icy!
Teddy He's obviously not here, is he?
Hilda Well, well, well. Oh, I have been remiss. But my business men take up so much of my time. I'll make some tea.

Cousin Hilda exits

Teddy Where'll he be, Henry?
Henry I don't know.
Teddy Which pub does he use?

Henry He doesn't go t'*Navigation* no more. He goes up t'hill mainly. Try *Stones'* pubs first, though.

Uncle Teddy and Mr Quell exit

Doris Mr Quell's paying you a visit. It's going to snow.

Cousin Hilda enters

Hilda It's mashing.
Doris They've gone looking.
Hilda Ee, I've failed you, Henry. I were satisfied wi' t'answers tha gave because I wanted to be satisfied. And I call mesen a Christian!
Doris And we had no idea anything like this was going on, Hilda. The state of the place. Poor boy.
Henry He were all right till Uncle Teddy sacked him.
Doris Uncle Teddy offered him a job out of the goodness of his heart. He had no need to. He kept him on as long as he possibly could, but he runs a business, not a charity. And your father didn't help himself either, the things he said about your Uncle Teddy's war effort.

Cousin Hilda sniffs

What's that supposed to mean?
Hilda What?
Doris That sniff. I distinctly heard you sniff.
Hilda I were breathing. I'll try not to do it in future, if it upsets you.
Doris You were insinuating that Teddy wasn't ready to do his bit. You were insinuating that his flat feet were a fraud.
Hilda There's lots I could say. I could say lots about folk having guilty consciences t'do wi' lad here. But I won't. I've been unChristian enough already. I'll get tea.

Cousin Hilda exits

Uncle Teddy and Mr Quell enter

Teddy Nowhere.
Doris Is it snowing?
Mr Quell It is snowing a little.
Doris Goodness. Well.
Mr Quell Is there anywhere else the boy could live, do you think?
Doris Oh well . . . we'll have him, won't we, Teddy? Of course we will, Mr Quell.

Slight pause while Uncle Teddy struggles

Teddy He obviously can't stay here, that's the first thing. And nobody could live with the sniffer.
Doris Not in front of the boy. I don't know, fancy drawing attention to her unpleasant nasal habit in front of a living relative.
Teddy (*to Doris*) You've made it worse by protesting about it. (*Publicly*) Well, of course, we'll have him, there's nowhere else, is there?

Doris (*hissing*) Teddy, you make it sound like a last resort!
Teddy (*aside*) You've done it again, Doris.
Doris We'll have him because we want to have him.

She embraces Henry but retreats quickly as she realizes he is about to wriggle free

Teddy I want the smallest room in the house. Where is it?
Henry T'i'n't in t'house for a kick off. Tha goes up entry two doors away into t'yard. Ours is t'second one on t'left, beyond t'midden. Torch is behind door.

Uncle Teddy exits, dismayed at these arrangements

Cousin Hilda enters

Hilda Tea's ready.
Doris It's all settled, Hilda. Henry's going to come and live with us.
Hilda Oh, but I were going to . . .

Pause

Please yoursen.
Mr Quell I do hope the snow isn't the harbinger of prolonged severe weather.
Hilda (*to Henry*) I'll come and build a snowman wi' tha if it is.

Uncle Teddy enters, shattered, with the torch still on

Doris What's the matter, Teddy, you look as if you've seen a ghost?
Teddy I've found him. He's in t'toilet. He's dead.

Very slight pause

Hilda Switch torch off. There's no point wasting batteries.

Music. The theme tune to "Music While You Work". Slide sequence into interval

SCENE 15

Music. Slide sequence

The Lights come up on a cocktail party at Uncle Teddy's and Aunty Doris's. Geoffrey and Daphne Porringer are there. Henry is very ill at ease in the midst of it

Teddy (*handing over a drink*) Geoffrey, a large gin and it.

Geoffrey Porringer, who receives the gin and it, is bluff, coarse and overbearing, punctuating the conversation with loud laughter

Geoffrey I like that dress you're almost wearing, Doris.
Doris Thank you, Geoffrey.
Teddy Watch him, Doris, they don't call him octopus arms for nothing.
Doris I'm sure Geoffrey is a perfect gentleman.
Geoffrey Daphne'll tell you how perfect I am, eh Daphne?
Daphne Geoffrey, you are a ... !

Daphne Porringer was going to say "one" but doesn't, not having the courage to finish her sentences. Doris, not able to bear the suspense has immediately dropped in the habit of finishing her sentences

Doris One? Are you having a holiday this year, Daphne?
Daphne Well, it is on the cards, of ...
Doris Course.
Daphne But Geoffrey decides. Geoffrey, isn't that ... ?
Doris Right. Yes, I suppose Teddy will insist on dragging me off to the south of France again. We named this house after our favourite hideaway, "Cap Ferrat".
Henry Will Uncle Teddy insist on dragging me to Cap Ferrat as well?
Doris Ah ...
Teddy We have to go in June, Henry. Circumstances dictate, more's the pity, and nothing must interfere with your education.
Geoffrey Don't want nipper cramping your style, and I don't mean sartorial, eh Doris?
Doris Really, Geoffrey.
Geoffrey We never had kids, of course. Couldn't trust Daphne with a tortoise, eh Daphne?
Daphne Oh Geoffrey, you know I'm ...
Doris Infertile?
Daphne Fond of animals.
Doris Your dress is very sweet, Daphne, did you make it yourself?
Daphne I did. It took me a long time because of my migraine.

Geoffrey She was at it all night, weren't you, Daphne? Sewing, I mean.

Daphne Geoffrey, you are a . . . !

Doris Isn't he just. Does Henry want a drink, Teddy?

Henry No thanks, Aunty Doris.

Geoffrey Oh, go on, give him a drink. The sooner you civilize them, the better.

Henry I'm quite civilized, thank you, Mr Porringer.

Doris Henry, is that the proper way to talk to an important business friend of Uncle Teddy's?

Teddy Geoffrey, how about lunch tomorrow? I've got some interesting goods coming in. Like to have a chat.

Geoffrey Tell me more.

Teddy Not here, Geoffrey, don't be daft, don't be daft.

Daphne Henry, we were very, very . . .

Doris Upset.

Daphne To hear about your . . .

Doris Father. He's a brave boy.

Teddy (*ruffling Henry's hair*) Oh, ay, he's a good lad.

Geoffrey You ought to take up boxing, put knots in that cotton.

Doris Geoffrey! It's hardly tactful to remind him he's flabby and not very muscular.

Teddy Doris always makes things worse by protesting about them.

Daphne I expect he'll be glad when he comes to the end of . . .

Doris Puberty?

Daphne The school holidays. You must miss your friends at Grammar School?

Teddy He's not going back to Thurmarsh.

Henry Aren't I?

Doris Oh, no, it's way over on t'other side of town. Too far to go every day now you're living with us.

Henry Where am I going?

Teddy Brasenose Preparatory School.

Henry Is that nearer?

Doris No travelling at all.

Teddy It's in Surrey.

Geoffrey That'll keep him out of your hair.

Doris Geoffrey!

Henry I like it at Thurmarsh Grammar.

Doris How can you say that? They threw him in the Rundle again last week. He'll be better not in the same town as that canal.

Henry Why is what's good for me always ruining my life?

Doris Henry, you don't think we don't . . . ?

Daphne Love you.

Doris glares

Music. Slide sequence

SCENE 16

*The Lights come up on Doris unpacking a holiday suitcase. She has a glass of
something by her*

Doris (*singing to herself*) "Every little breeze seems to whisper Louise, da,
da, da, da, da, dee, da, da, da, da ... I love you, Louise ..."
Cousin Hilda enters. She sniffs
Cousin Hilda! We've only just got back.
Hilda (*sniffing*) Oh ay.
Doris Teddy!
Hilda Tha needn't call for reinforcements. (*She sniffs*) I don't approve.
Doris (*misunderstanding and looking at her unpacking*) Is it my fault Teddy's
business meeting was in the south of France in a sun-soaked holiday
resort?!
Hilda I were speaking about Henry. I don't approve of giving folks ideas.
Doris We have to move with the times, Hilda.
Henry Why?
Doris Pardon?
Hilda Was a time tha'd've said "tha what?", not "pardon?"
Doris If you've spent hard-earned cash on two trams and a bus to come
here for a ding-dong you're in for a disappointment, Hilda.
Hilda I didn't mean to be unChristian.
Doris Henry is doing very well at Brasenose Preparatory, excellent reports.
Hilda He's wrote home. To me.
Doris Oh, has he? He writes to us every week. Only a page, of course. But he
never misses.
Hilda (*producing it*) This is four pages. Wi' no gaps. Both sides.

Aunty Doris takes the letter and begins reading it

Henry enters and speaks his letter to Cousin Hilda

Henry "Caning teaches you respect for authority, that's what Mr A.B.
Noon BA, our headmaster, said, so we should be grateful. I said thank
you afterwards but I don't think I meant it. They call it thrashing here.
You'll never believe the nickname I've been given, it's amusing. I'm Oiky.
Oiky Pratt. Of course, my surname is a hoot on its own. I don't mind
though, honest. Last week there were ... was a craze for telling fortunes
but it's over now. Everytime I had a go they said I'm going to be a sewage-
worker, or a lavatory attendant. The fellows like jokes. My cricket scores
are a bit disappointing. Nought, nought, nought, nought, nought not out,
nought, did not bat, retired hurt nought, nought, nought not out, nought
and nought. But I'm pleased my form's consistent. The debating society
arranged a mock election thing which was fun. Conservatives, three
hundred and sixty-four, Labour, one. The bruises are almost gone now
and it's simply ages since I had a dead thrush in my bed ..."

Henry exits

Doris (*surreptitiously blowing her nose*) He should have told us, silly boy.

Hilda (*momentarily giving her the benefit of the doubt*) Why, what would tha have done?

Doris Been sympathetic, of course. We all have problems pulling ourselves up in the world.

Hilda (*exploding with anger*) It's a wicked shame, that's what it is! Tha can doll thaself up with tha fancy this and tha fancy that but our Henry's norra settee! Tha can't dress up his little heart and soul wi' accessories. Dormitories and such like! He should come back to Thurmarsh Grammar.

Doris Oh, should he? May I speak? I do have some experience in the ways of the world ...

Teddy enters

Teddy Doris! Ready or not! (*Seeing Hilda*) Aah! Hallo, Cousin Hilda.

Hilda I'm here on account of it were on me conscience about leaving lad to tender mercies of his father in Paradise Lane. I don't scruple to admit it, unlike some.

Teddy I want to give him every advantage.

Hilda So tha should! It were tha sacking his father were t'death of him!

Doris How dare you draw attention to my husband's deepest guilt feelings?!

Teddy Doris!

Doris (*screaming at Cousin Hilda and forgetting to talk posh*) Tha can just get out of here, tha interfering old cow!

Teddy Doris!

Doris Tha hasn't seen her! Upsetting me, trying to come between Henry and us!

Hilda Well, well. Where's tha "I'm just talkin to t'vicar", voice now then?

Doris (*wounded to the quick*) Oh, oh! Teddy, Teddy, say something, before I forget meself.

Teddy Now then, ladies ...

Hilda Save tha breath to cool tha porridge. I'll show mesen out. (*With utter contempt, unable to keep it in*) Ezra were nowt but a scranny, self-pitying drunk but he were salt o'the earth compared to you pair. God help Henry.

Doris You're as jealous as sin, Hilda.

Hilda Jealous?

Doris Mr Right never did come along, did he?

Hilda claps her hand to her mouth and runs out

Pause

We have to consider termination at Brasenose.

Teddy Don't talk daft. Doris, forget it, will you, you look like a Gorgon.

She stares at him in horror

Music. Slide sequence

SCENE 17

Tram sounds. Henry is on one, a girl is sitting next to him

Mabel Hallo.

Pause

Hey, cloth-ears, I'm talking to you.

Henry Oh, I was miles away.

Mabel No, tha weren't, tha were sitting next to me. Was that amusing? I'm practising being witty. Tha goes to Thurmarsh Grammar School for Boys, don't tha?

Henry No.

Mabel I've seen you. I go to Thurmarsh Grammar School for Girls.

Henry I go to Brasenose Preparatory School in Surrey.

Mabel Tha's havin' us on.

Henry I used to go to Thurmarsh Grammar School for Boys.

Mabel I knew tha did. Tha talks a bit posh, don't tha?

Henry Oh, I'm sorry. I forget. It's a habit. I'm on me holiday now.

Mabel I go to North Wales coast.

Henry I meant I'm home on school holiday.

Mabel I know, it were a witticism. What tha got in t'bag?

Henry Oh, nowt much. A bottle of Tizer, a packet of Mintoes and a lucky bag.

Conductor (*calling out*) Brunswick!

Mabel Oops, this is me stop.

Henry I used to go to Brunswick Road Primary School.

Mabel Geraround, don't tha? I'm Mabel Billington. Tha were in my horoscope for today, "an interesting stranger".

Henry (*pleased*) Nice to meet you, Mabel, I'm Henry Pratt.

Mabel I've had a chat with Henry Pratt. Laugh, will tha! That's a witty remark. Tara.

She exits

The tram continues

Conductor (*calling out*) Paradise!

Pause

Paradise!

Slight pause. The tram continues

(*To Henry*) I thought tha wanted Paradise Lane?

Henry No, sorry. I've changed my mind. (*He starts on his picnic*)

Pause. Then music. Slide sequence

SCENE 18

The Lights come up on Aunty Doris entertaining Geoffrey Porringer. They are clearly quite intimate, Geoffrey laughing suggestively. They spring apart, flustered, as ...

Henry enters. He doesn't notice anything

Henry Good-afternoon, Mr Porringer.
Geoffrey Well, Doris, I'm sorry I missed Teddy.
Doris Oh, you're leaving, Geoffrey. Yes, it was unfortunate Teddy wasn't here. What am I to tell him?

Geoffrey is mystified at first but then realizes it is for Henry's benefit

Geoffrey Tell him, Bingley can't cope. We'll have to explore other avenues. (*To Henry*) Cheer up, it might never happen.

Geoffrey exits

Doris Mr Porringer dropped by to see Teddy. You know, on business. Thinking that Teddy might be here. Because sometimes he is about this time. Am I flushed? Tedious business, business. Funnily enough, I was particularly hoping Teddy would be home early because we are going out this evening, to a club.
Henry (*excited*) Oh, I've never been to a club.
Doris You'll be all right, will you?
Henry Aren't I going?
Doris It's Rawlaston Working Men's club, Henry, not the *Moulin Rouge*, more's the pity.
Henry You never take me anywhere!
Doris You're under-age, dear.
Henry Excuses, excuses! I'm not as green as I'm cabbage-looking! You just don't like having me with you! That's why you always take your holidays in France during term-time. Concern for my education, my foot!
Doris (*on the verge of tears*) You don't like me very much, do you?
Henry I want to! I want to! But you won't let me into your life!

Music. Slide sequence

SCENE 19

The Lights come up. Club sounds. Uncle Teddy, Aunty Doris and Henry are seated at a table. On a small stage a very bad, and very drunk magician, the Amazing Illingworth, is staggering through his act

Henry Don't forget Geoffrey Porringer's message, Aunty Doris.
Doris (*choking on her drink and then, about the Amazing Illingworth*) Oh, I'd love to know how they do that? He's really very talented.

The magician, to his great pleasure and amazement, overhears this

Henry Uncle Teddy, I think you've been done at Brasenose Preparatory.

Teddy Done? What d'you mean done?

Henry You're paying out lots of money, but the education's worse than it was at Thurmarsh Grammar, which is free.

Teddy Later, Henry. (*To Doris*) What's this about Geoffrey Porringer?

Doris Oh ... um ... he popped round to the house this afternoon. With a message. (*About the magician*) Oh look, Henry, isn't that ... interesting?!

Henry You can see how he does it.

The magician overhears this as well

Uncle Teddy, perhaps next term you'd get better value for money if I went back to Thurmarsh Grammar.

Teddy Brasenose is a preparatory school. You aren't there to be educated. You're there to be prepared. (*To Doris*) Why couldn't Geoffrey Porringer have rung me at the office?

Doris I don't know, I'm not a mind reader.

Henry Perhaps it was a secret, the message. It sounded pretty secret.

Doris Drink your orange squash, Henry.

Compère (*unseen*) Thank you, the Amazing Illingworth.

The magician exits reluctantly as he hadn't finished

Before I announce next act, will the bar please not serve the Amazing Illingworth any more. And now melody. The next turn has asked me to apologize for her very bad cold, but she says she won't let her audience down. I told her we wouldn't be disappointed but she's very game. So let's hear it for the Tadcaster Thrush.

Sporadic applause

The Tadcaster Thrush enters, a club singer in a low-cut dress with a red nose. She sings, "Confidentially", nasally, occasionally losing her voice altogether

Henry What am I being prepared for at Brasenose, Uncle Teddy?

Teddy Dalton. What was Geoffrey Porringer's message then, Doris?

Doris Oh, I can't remember.

Henry Dalton?

Teddy He brings me a message so secret and so important that he can't phone me at the office, and you forget it?

Doris Shh! You'll put the artiste off.

Pause to appreciate "Confidentially"

Henry What's Dalton?

Doris We can't discuss it here.

Another few golden notes from the Tadcaster Thrush

Teddy Doris, summat's up.

Doris Just because I've forgotten a silly message!

Henry (*helpfully*) I remember the message.

Doris You wanted to know about Dalton, dear, well Dalton is actually one of the best public schools in the country. You'll love it there, Henry, a kind thoughtful boy, like you.

Teddy Tell us this message then.

Henry It was "Bingley can't cope. We'll have to explore other avenues."

Teddy I don't understand it. What the hell does he mean, "Bingley"?

Henry Perhaps it was in code?

A slight pause

Teddy Ay, that'll be it.

Henry Pretty useless code if no-one understands it.

Teddy I think I've got a fair idea of what it means now, thank you, Henry.

Henry Where is Dalton?

Teddy In Somerset.

Henry I don't want to go to Somerset, I don't want to go to Dalton, I don't want to go to a public school! (*Henry falls into a massive sulk*)

The Tadcaster Thrush gives up in a spate of coughing and exits

A dribble of applause

Compère (*unseen*) Thank you little lady, I'm sure we all agree she'd be best to go straight home and put her head over a bowl of Friar's Balsam. And here's an announcement I should have done at t'beginning but in view of the Amazing Illingworth's condition I forgot. With great regret I have to inform you of the death of one of our members, Bill Oldfield. We've sent all our sympathies to Madge and the family. Funeral's on Tuesday. And now comedy. I give you, Talwyn Jones, the Celtic Droll.

Henry brightens, instantly enthralled and applauding enthusiastically. Uncle Teddy and Aunty Doris sink, their heads in their hands

Music. Slide sequence

SCENE 20

The Lights come up on Dalton College and Henry meeting Paul Hargreaves, a sophisticated, upper middle-class, Hampstead boy. Henry is utterly dejected

Paul Who are you fagging for?

Henry The notice said Lampo Davey, and Tosser Pilkington-Brick.

Paul Tosser Pilkington-Brick! He's only the captain of the rugby team and the cricket team, and, apparently, one of the best sportsmen Dalton's had for years.

Henry Oh.

Paul My father used to be here so he tends to be in the know.

Henry Is your father a school-teacher?

Paul Good Lord, no! He's a brain surgeon, old chap.

Henry (*thinking he's joking*) Oh. And mine's a test pilot.

Paul (*taking him literally*) Jolly good.
Henry I like jokes.
Paul Jolly good. You must tell me one sometime. Do you know anybody here?
Henry I only know one boy. He was at Brasenose as well.
Paul Brasenose?
Henry It's in Surrey. His name is Tubman-Edwards, only I can't stand him, and he feels the same about me, times ten.
Paul That's a shame. What form are you in?
Henry One-A.
Paul So am I. It's the bright form. I'm Paul Hargreaves.
Henry I'm Henry Pratt.

A slight pause

Paul Pratt. (*Seeing another boy offstage*) Hooper, come and meet Pratt. He's from the north but his father's a test pilot.
Henry Is your father really a brain surgeon?
Paul (*surprised*) Yes.

Tosser Pilkington-Brick enters

I say that's Tosser Pilkington-Brick.
Tosser All new bugs to the shower. Regulation circumcisions in twenty minutes.

Paul and Henry look at each other

Music. Slide sequence

SCENE 21

Sounds of birds and a cricket match

Lampo Davey is with Henry. Lampo is a self-consciously effete and artistic eighteen-year-old

Lampo Bullying is the last refuge of the inadequate. You should say that to them.
Henry Will it help?
Lampo No, but you'll feel superior when your head's down the lavatory. However you can rest easy in my company, young Pratt.
Henry Shall I tell you a joke, Lampo? I'll tell you about my aunty. She had a mangle. I wouldn't say my aunty was ugly but I was talking to the mangle for five minutes before I realized it wasn't her.

He laughs. Lampo doesn't. Applause for the cricket, off

I think I understand what it is I lack in sport now, Lampo, speed, accuracy, control, strength, skill and talent.
Lampo My, you are developing a personality! Shall we lounge on the

sward? The English summer is quite dreadful, the banality of all that bright green. Compare it with Tuscany, Pratt.
Henry Oh, absolutely, compared with Tuscany.

Lampo is pleased. Applause, off

Shot, Tosser!
Lampo (*not pleased*) Oh, Henry Pratt, why crown ye yon hero with laurels so many? D'you know that Tosser eats that chocolate drink you buy for him, in powder form, with a teaspoon. He's disgusting. Heigho. I am the most sensitive, subtle and artistic eighteen-year-old in Orange House. Which isn't saying much. Oh, that sports field! See the many-headed Hydra of common humanity crawl and throb! You are an original, Pratt. So am I, of course. Quaintly enough, when I first met you, I thought, "Oh dear, clueless, clotto." I didn't even think you were remotely pretty. But now I quite like my fatty little faggy-chops.

He puts his hand on Henry's knee, intimately. Henry is horribly embarrassed and shocked

Henry Don't do that, please! I thought you said I'd be safe with you.
Lampo I've shocked you. Enough of confuse-a-fag for one day.

Lampo exits

Applause and cheers off, Henry joins in

Tosser enters with a cricket bat, mopping his brow

Tosser Hallo, Pratt! My fifth lost ball this term. It's the waiting about that's so tiresome. Nip down to the town, would you, I've run out of that hair oil stuff. (*He gives him some money*)
Voice (*in the distance off*) I say, Tosser!
Tosser What! And about time, chaps! Exert yourself, Pratt.

Tosser exits with determined nonchalance

Henry stands looking at the money in his hand

Music. Slide sequence

SCENE 22

The Lights come up on Lampo in his study

Henry enters

Lampo I didn't say come in.
Henry You didn't say, "Stay out".
Lampo I couldn't, mime is silent.
Henry What were you doing?
Lampo Nothing titillating. I'm appearing in the end of summer term concert. I'm doing a satirical mime entitled, "Sir Stafford Cripps in the

Underworld". Or "Austerity in Post-War Britain, is it Hell on Earth?"
Shall I stun you with a morsel?

Henry Mm.

*Lampo concentrates and then launches himself into a series of small, preten-
tious and incomprehensible gestures*

Lampo That is, of course, only the middle section.

Henry It's very good, Lampo. I'm doing an act too. It's entitled, "Henry,
Ee-by-gum, I am daft, Pratt". It's going to be comic.

Lampo You've rendered me speechless. Dear boy, nobody below fourth
year ever does a solo.

Tosser enters

Tosser I could eat a stallion.

Lampo How I envy your simple appetites. Prick and belly, and you smile
contentedly.

Tosser You know me, Lampo.

Lampo Well young Pratt, is his fry-up fried? Are his beans baked?

Henry I ... er ... there isn't any food.

Lampo You can't have dropped our money down a drain again?

Tosser Pratt, this is a pretty poor show. What's the matter with you?

Henry (*quietly*) I'm living a lie.

Tosser Did he say, he's living a lie?

Henry I've got to tell you something awful.

Tosser What is it, Pratt?

Henry My father isn't a test pilot. My father made penknives, and died
sitting on the outside lats.

Lampo Good Lord, you mean you're an actual slum kid!

Henry It wasn't a slum, it was sub-standard housing.

Tosser What's this got to do with our provisions?

Henry Tubman-Edwards was at Brasenose and I have to give him money
and other things so he won't tell the whole school I'm a cowardly liar and
a fraud.

Lampo Oh, how vile little boys can be!

Tosser What a blighter! What an arch cad! He's the coward, Pratt.

Henry cries

Lampo Oh for goodness sake, don't blatt.

Tosser Well done, for having the courage to spill the beans. You'll have to
tell the truth to the whole house and face the music though. As for your
tormentor, well, when I see Tubman-Edwards he'll wish he'd thought
twice!

Lampo It was pathetic of you to use the same lie six times about dropping
our money down a drain.

Tosser Well, Lampo, it's the refectory or starve.

Tosser exits

Henry is beaming

Lampo I can tell you adore him.

Henry Did tha ever read *Biggles*, Lampo?

Lampo *Biggles*!?

Henry When tha were little?

Lampo I was never little.

Henry I, Algy, and Tosser, Biggles, united against the filthy hun, Tubman-Edwards! (*He puts his hands to his eyes as if they were goggles and makes loud, enthusiastic machine-gun noises*) Duga dugga dugga dugga dugga dugga ... !

Henry exits

Lampo Oh dear, condescension does have its drawbacks.

Music. Slide sequence

Scene 23

The Lights come up on a picnic on the river

Henry is with Paul Hargreaves, Mr and Mrs Hargreaves and their daughter, Diana

Mrs Hargreaves You like China tea, do you, Henry?

Henry Very much, Mrs Hargreaves.

Mrs Hargreaves Are you post-lacterian?

Henry No, I'm Church of England.

Paul Ass. Post-lacterian means you like the milk in last.

Henry I like the milk in first.

Diana So do I.

Paul No, you don't.

Diana You don't know anything about me. I didn't know you'd be coming out to tea with us, Henry.

Paul (*aside to Henry*) My sister's got a crush on you. Yawn, yawn.

Mrs Hargreaves You must come and visit us, Henry.

Mr Hargreaves Have you ever been to Hampstead?

Henry Yes.

Paul Liar.

Diana D'you know, across the road from us there's this potty professor of history who's frightfully intellectual but practically gaga and we've got a quite famous artist living next door but he's painted himself out.

Mr Hargreaves There's an excellent new post impressionist exhibition on at the Tate, Paul.

Henry Does "post impressionism" mean you like the sugar in last?

Pause. He is stared at

It was a joke. Like post-lacterian.

Paul Henry is a budding comedian.

Laughter

Mr Hargreaves I hear we are to see our budding comedian in action this
evening?

Diana Are you nervous, Henry?

Paul (*aside to Henry*) You're gawping at Diana, ass.

Mrs Hargreaves (*taking the minutest bite from a tiny sandwich*) Oh Henry, it
is good to meet you. I'm so glad Paul is broadening his knowledge of
people.

Slides and music

SCENE 24

The Lights come up on the end of term concert

*Lampo and Henry are in the wings waiting to go on, Lampo in a toga and
laurel wreath, Henry holding his costume*

Lampo I'm leaving this philistine country, Henry. I intend to live where I
will be appreciated, Crete.

Henry I'm spending the holidays abroad with the Hargreaves family this
summer. Paul's sister Diana, will be there.

Lampo I do wish you could have been my bit of rough, little slum boy.
Sorry, sub-standard housing boy. But I understand why. The working
classes have always hated homosexuality. My cue coming up.

Henry "Sir Stafford Cripps in the Underworld."

Lampo I'm not sure school is ready for political satire expressed in modern
dance. Heigh-ho. Henry, if you ever change your mind, let me know.

Henry Yes, Lampo. I promised Tosser I'd let him know as well.

*Lampo, more than piqued, exits with a theatrical toss of the head. The
"Baccarole" from "Orpheus in the Underworld" swells up. Lampo does his
turn which involves lots of running about and "Isadora Duncan" type flowing
movements with a sheet. The act is totally incomprehensible*

Lampo (*to Henry as he comes off stage*) They're peasants, you should do
well.

Lampo exits

Tosser steps on to the school stage

Tosser And next, boys and members of staff, he's only in his second year,
but he has tremendous courage, here he is, young Henry "Ee-by-gum I
am daft" Pratt!

*Henry comes on to the school hall stage wearing a mortar board and gown and
a comic false nose and moustache of the joke-shop variety. The audience greet
him warmly*

Henry 'Ow do. I'm t'new headmaster, tha knows. My name's Oiky Pratt

MA. I were born in a slum. I were. I come from a slum. Me dad, one day, he said to me, "Henry . . ." —he were clever that way, 'cos it's me name— Henry", he said, "I've gorra pain in me eye." I didn't ask him which one. He only had one. He couldn't afford two. "Henry", he said again, 'cos his memory was still quite good in them days, "Henry, get eye drops and gerrus dinner at same time." I opened t'oven door, and there was this great big rat. I said, "Dad, there's a great big rat in t'oven." He said, "That's funny, I only ordered a little 'un." I won't say we were poor, but I didn't have mumps. I had mump. We could only afford one. Ee by gum, I am daft.

As his act comes to an end, music swells up, "There'll Always Be An England."
Slide of a photograph reminiscent of Henry's father

SCENE 25

The Lights come up on Aunty Doris meeting Henry, who is removing his costume

Doris Henry!

Henry Hallo, Aunty Doris! You didn't tell me you were coming. What a nice surprise. Did you see my act?

Doris No, I didn't. I——

Henry Aunty Doris, it were the greatest moment of my life! I told a joke about a rat, and a joke about a mangle and . . . what? What's happened, Aunty Doris?

Doris Teddy's got problems. Business problems. He's got problems with his English end. He's going to have to wind it up. Do you understand what I'm saying?

Henry Well, yes, he's going to have to wind up his English end.

Doris I'm saying he's gone out east to try to preserve his oriental end. If he can hang on to that, all may not be lost. Do you understand what I'm saying?

Henry Well, yes, he's going to hang on to his oriental end.

Doris I'm saying he's going to have to live in Rangoon. And I, being his wife, co-habiting with him, will therefore naturally live . . . with him . . . in Rangoon. We have a small, one-bedroom company flat there. Do you understand what I'm saying?

Henry Well, yes, I'm going to have to sleep on the floor.

Doris That wouldn't be very satisfactory, would it? Our adopted and much-loved son having to sleep on the floor. We couldn't have that. Therefore you cannot exactly . . . live with us . . . in Rangoon.

Henry Well, of course, I can't. I go to school here.

Doris We're almost ruined. The receiver will take the money for "Cap Ferrat". I don't mind for us. We've had a good innings. Uncle Teddy always says, "You can't lose money, unless you've made it." But . . . do you understand what I'm saying?

Henry Well, yes, I won't be able to go to France with the Hargreaves?
Doris I'm saying we can't afford to send you here any more. You're going back to Thurmarsh Grammar.
Henry But Aunty Doris . . . !
Doris You liked it there. You didn't want to leave.
Henry Yes, but . . . things are different now!
Doris Everything's different now!
Henry Yes, but where will I live?
Doris We wouldn't send you out of the family. You'll live with Cousin Hilda, of course.

Music. Slides

SCENE 26

The Lights come up on Cousin Hilda and Henry

Hilda Mrs Wedderburn has very kindly lent you her camp bed. I hope you're very grateful to Mrs Wedderburn?
Henry Yes, I am . . . (*He coughs*) . . . I'm very grateful to Mrs Wedderburn.
Hilda You'll have to share my room.
Henry Share your . . . ! (*He is overtaken by an explosion of coughing*)
Hilda That's a bad cough, tha's got, Henry. Any road, we'll have to see how we get on. There's nowt else for it. If it's not satisfactory, I'll give Mr Carpenter notice. He's a journalist. (*She sniffs*) I know Teddy and Doris were spendin' money as what I don't have but I were never happy about tha being sent to them schools, our Henry. Getting ideas. Still, how the mighty have fallen, but I mustn't be unChristian. (*She sniffs and then hands him a book wrapped in brown paper*) It's just a little thing. I know what a great one tha is for reading. I were just saying to Mrs Wedderburn, "I don't know where he gets it from, but it's a pleasure to see him wi' his nose buried in all them words."
Henry (*half to himself*) I read with my eyes, Hilda, not my nose.
Hilda Tha what?
Henry Nothing.
Hilda I hope it's all right for thee. She said she'd be happy to change it if it wasn't soiled.
Henry I'll make sure I wash my hands before I read it.
Hilda Is tha all right? Tha's not got a fever, 'as tha?
Henry I'm fine, Cousin Hilda.
Hilda Come on then, hurry up and open it.

Reluctantly, Henry opens the parcel

Henry (*reading*) *Biggles Scours the Jungle.*

A slight pause

Hilda Well . . . (*She sniffs*)
Henry It's marvellous, it really is the best present you could have given me, Cousin Hilda.

Hilda Open it.
Henry (*doing so and reading*) "Welcome home, Henry.".
Hilda This is your home now.

Pause. Henry runs out

Henry! Where's tha off to wi' that cold?
Henry (*calling, off*) I'll be back for my tea.
Hilda It's brawn, tha likes brawn.

Music. Slides

SCENE 27

Tram sounds. The Lights come up on Henry, Mabel Billington and the conductor

Tram sounds. Henry is sitting on a tram, looking ill. Mabel Billington is reading, and not noticing him

Henry (*mumbling*) . . . Pain . . . pain in me eye. He only had one, he couldn't afford two. Dad! I'll get tea, Dad. Traitor, traitor! Our Henry! Rats in the mangle . . . (*He opens his eyes wide, staring*) . . . I am with thee, my son!
Conductor (*calling*) Paradise!

Henry stands unsteadily, eyes staring

Been on t'booze a bit early, hasn't tha lad?
Henry I've had a religious experience on this tram.
Mabel Hallo, interesting stranger. I were keepin' me head down 'cause I thought tha'd flipped tha lid till tha explained.
Hilda You saw me in your stars.
Mabel That were years ago, now I've learnt that astrology is the devil's food for unChristian appetites. This is all knowledge we need, in't it? (*She holds up her book, which is a bible*)
Conductor Bloody hell, two of 'em.
Mabel God must have arranged whole situation.
Henry I'm like Paul on t'road to Damascus.
Conductor Weren't Bob Hope and Bing Crosby in that? Canal Bridge!
Henry I'm on t'verge of cleansing mysen in t'sacred waters of t'stinking Rundle. Nobody need push me in, neither.
Conductor Tha daft lummock, tha's got a flamin' high temperature!

Henry exits

Mabel (*calling after him*) I remember you, Henry Pratt. Why don't tha join church youth club? I'm secretary. (*Smiling at the Conductor*) Since God came into my life my self-confidence has bloomed!
Conductor (*non-plussed and depressed*) Ee, lass, heaven help thy mother.

A large splash and slurping sound, off

Music. Slides

SCENE 28

Country sounds. Henry and Mabel Billington are hiking. She has a rucksack.
They arrive at the top of a hill

Mabel Phew, I am hot in these hiking boots. It's been a grand walk, Henry.
We mustn't be late back for choir practice, though.
Henry Oh no. Why don't you take your hiking boots off?
Mabel Ay, I will. I'll take my oil-skin off as well.

Henry turns away, overcome with physical excitement

What's tha doing?
Henry That's Drobwell Main Colliery down there.
Mabel Tha what? Phew, I am hot. I'll have to take one of my jumpers off as
well.
Henry (*talking, at first to hide his excitement and embarrassment, then to
impress Mabel*) God's been very good to me this term, Mabel. He's let me
pass nine O levels, Latin, English, English Literature, French, Maths,
Advanced Maths, Geography, History and Physics.
Mabel Didn't tha take scripture?
Henry No, it wasn't on the syllabus. I'm studying it in my spare time,
though.
Mabel Oh good. Oh phew, I am hot.
Henry Mabel, why don't we take God to Africa together?
Mabel Oh all right, we'll travel up the rivers by boat.
Henry We'll come to a village. The natives have blowpipes, but they're
friendly.
Mabel They've never heard of Christianity.
Henry All the women have bare ... breasts.
Mabel We'll soon put a stop to that.
Henry Oh ay, yeah. They're sacrificing a goat. It's a fertility rite.
Mabel We'll save them from their pagan rituals.
Henry Then after a hard day's saving, we'll go back to our own hut. We'll
go to bed early.
Mabel Definitely, I need my eight hours.
Henry We'll go to bed at ten and get up at seven.
Mabel (*working it out, then*) No, that's nine hours.
Henry We need an hour before we go to sleep.
Mabel What for?
Henry You know.
Mabel Oh, ay, reading t'bible.
Henry Oh, ay, in that case we'll have to go to bed at nine.
Mabel Phew, I am hot.

Mabel is enjoying the sun. Henry puts out a tentative hand to stroke her.
Mabel thinks it is an insect and swats at the hand. Henry repeats the gesture
and Mabel swats his hand again. Henry repeats the gesture. Mabel suddenly
realizes that it's him. She brings her rucksack down on his head, hard

Henry Ow! What did you do that for!?

Mabel What were tha doing? I thought tha were a gnat.

Henry I fancy you.

Mabel I thought tha were religious!

Henry I am religious, I'm also a man. Religious people have sex, you know.

Mabel I never will. I'm saving my body for God. It's a sin any road, if tha's not married.

Henry God is forgiving.

Mabel That's not meant to be an excuse for sinning all over the place. I think that stuff's awful. I were nearly sick in sex education.

Henry But God created all that. He wouldn't have created it if he meant you to be nearly sick in sex education.

Mabel He didn't create it for having fun. He created it for having babies. If he'd created it for fun he'd have designed it a lot better than what he did. It's quite obvious to me, Henry, that I have been placed in your path as a temptation. So until you're spiritually stronger I think it's best that we only meet in a crowded room. Goodbye.

Mabel Billington exits

A very loud siren, which changes the mood

Mr Quell enters

Mr Quell It's Henry.

Henry Mr Quell.

Mr Quell Twenty-seven hours, they've been trapped down that mine. One of them was brought up dead. Sixteen years old and dead.

Henry Why did God kill him, Mr Quell?

Mr Quell God didn't. Suffocation did. Pit props did. And an inadequate mining survey did. That seam was due to close in three weeks.

Henry I'm having terrible doubts about my faith. I think I think one thing and then I find I think the exact opposite. I know it is better to be generous than to be mean, to be kind rather than cruel, and to try to have faith in man's capacity to overcome the evil in his own nature. I'm finding it difficult, Mr Quell.

Mr Quell These matters aren't easy.

Henry I thought I'd had my own message from God. I thought I saw my dead father pointing an accusing foggy finger at me through a tram window. Mr Quell, I felt so guilty I actually jumped into the Rundle Canal, the holy waters of Thurmarsh. Own message! God may have spoken to St Theresa but what I heard was the voice of a viral infection.

Mr Quell You're looking washed out, Henry Pratt. You're not masturbating yourself to death, are you?

Henry I've completely given up self-abuse, Mr Quell.

Mr Quell Really? That's an achievement. Perhaps you found purity as well as wisdom in the Yorkshire Ganges.

The siren sounds loudly again. Music. Slides. 1951 to 1953

SCENE 29

Pub noises. Miss Candy is sitting hidden by a newspaper

Hilda and Henry enter

Hilda Your Uncle Frank and Aunty Kate said they'd be here, in t'pub. We're on t'early side.

Henry I never thought I'd live to see the day you'd set foot in a pub, Cousin Hilda. Shall I sit on t'step outside, while you sup up?

Hilda Enough o'your cheek. This is different. It's rustic.

Miss Candy (*from behind her paper*) And I'm a country bumpkin, eh?

Henry Miss Candy!

She puts her paper down

Hilda, it's Miss Candy!

Miss Candy Well! It's Henry Pratt! Let me look at you. Well, well, well. Ezra, that's what I called you. You hated that.

Henry I've been called worse things since. At my boarding schools down south I was known as "Oiky" and when I went back to Thurmarsh Grammar I was called "Snobby".

Miss Candy Nothing like personal abuse for building character, eh?

Henry Oh, it's super to see you! You look just the same.

Miss Candy Nonsense. My moustache has gone grey. (*She laughs*) Pints for both of you?

Hilda sniffs in horror

Henry Cousin Hilda's my parent now. She'll have a lemonade.

Miss Candy Jolly good. This is my corner, Henry. Here I sit and merge in with all the other antiques. I'm retired now. They got rid of me. But I've kept my motor bike.

Henry I still haven't met anyone quite like you.

Miss Candy Thank goodness? I wouldn't wish my face on anyone, eh Hilda?

She laughs again. Hilda sniffs

I have lived a very dull life. Oh but Henry, my very special Henry, do tell me you're a rebellious poet? Or a brilliant scientist in the making?

Henry I'm pretty average, really.

Miss Candy Ah. Do any of us manage to get through this vale of tears without self-delusions, eh, Hilda?

Hilda Henry Pratt isn't tha just tha father's son. Yon teacher wants to know results of her labours. Say summat. Impressive. Stuff as what I don't understand.

Henry Knock me down with feather, I do believe my adoptive parent is praising me.

Hilda Ee, where's tha respect?

Henry All right. I'll tell you my politics.

Hilda I didn't mean that, tha know's what I think o'folks wi'opinions.

Henry You're in a pub now, Cousin Hilda, you're allowed. I believe a brain surgeon should earn less than a dustman, because the brain surgeon's job is intrinsically more rewarding.

Hilda Well at least drivel sounds better wi'a few long words in't.

Miss Candy Oh, but he's a radical. Lovely! Mad! But a radical.

Henry Do you realize the Conservatives lost the nineteen forty-five election on purpose because they knew whatever party got in stood no chance? That what Reg Hammond reckons, Cousin Hilda.

Hilda That Reg Hammond has a lot to answer for.

Henry You see, Miss Candy, the British middle class is simply scared of Labour ...

Hilda Thank you Henry. We've had enough for a while. That was very nice.

Miss Candy (*unable to articulate the depths of her feelings*) Ah Henry. Do ... It's ... Oh yes, indeed. I'm just a very ancient romantic, I suppose.

Henry D'you remember when you asked me to tell you what people said about you?

Miss Candy Yes! How I wished it had all been true! Stripping in Wakefield might have been quite exciting.

Hilda chokes

And wasn't I supposed to drink a bottle of gin a day?

Hilda has indigestion

Couldn't afford to, eh Hilda? But I did love a Yank, who went home and left me broken-hearted.

Hilda Oh, I'm sorry.

Miss Candy (*to Hilda*) Oh, don't be. She came back.

Hilda is stunned but very quiet

Strange, isn't it? I mean, the one unusual thing in my entire life was that I loved a woman, and you all missed it! (*She laughs*) Oh dear. My friend is very particular about time, so I must go. (*To Hilda*) My friend doesn't like pubs either. Well, Henry ...

Henry Goodbye, Miss Candy.

Miss Candy exits

Hilda Frank and Kate aren't coming. I haven't been honest wi' tha about pub.

Henry Cousin Hilda, d'you mean, you have frequented ale houses before!

Hilda Give over. No, I don't like shocks, I don't like surprises mesen. I had a reason for wanting to come to Rowth Bridge.

Aunty Doris enters

Henry Aunty Doris!

Hilda I wanted you to meet landlady.

Doris Hilda! Henry! I dreaded this might happen. But I always knew it would.

Hilda It had to be done, Doris.

Henry (*to Aunty Doris*) What are you doing here?

Doris It's a long story, perhaps best not told.

Henry Where's Teddy? When did you come back from Rangoon?

Doris We never went to Rangoon. I've been here three years. Cousin Hilda knew.

Henry What about Teddy?

Doris Teddy's in prison.

Henry Prison!

Hilda Shh! Nobody here knows.

Doris That woman's a saint, Henry, I always said.

Henry (*quieter*) Prison! What for?

Doris Business offences. You know. Tax evasion. Fraud. Theft. Receiving stolen goods. Business offences. He didn't want you to know.

Hilda Ay, at least he had the decency to feel terribly ashamed of hissen in front of you, Henry.

Doris (*crying*) I'm sorry. He comes out next year.

Henry But you wrote to me from Rangoon.

Doris I forwarded them to a friend, he sent them on.

Henry I know who it was. Geoffrey Porringer.

Geoffrey Porringer enters

Geoffrey Speaking of me. And how are you, young sir?

Henry Hallo, Geoffrey.

Geoffrey Don't make it so hard for yourself. Life, I mean. Let's be brutally honest. What did Uncle Teddy ever do for you?

Doris Geoffrey!

Henry He took me into his home and treated me like a son to the best of his abilities.

Geoffrey Only because he felt guilty because he thought he caused your father's death by sacking him.

Doris Geoffrey! He doesn't know his father hanged himself.

A slight pause

Hilda Ee Doris, tha always did make things worse by protesting about them.

A slight pause

Geoffrey Hilda, if you come through into the bar parlour, I'll give you a short, you look as though you could do with it.

Hilda A short what?

Geoffrey (*bewildered, then, to Henry*) Come on smile, it might never happen.

Geoffrey exits

Pause. The two women look at Henry

Billy The Half-Wit enters, sorting his coins

Billy Only a pint. Two on a Saturday. Frank Turnbull's very strict about it.
Henry Billy! Billy!
Billy I don't know thee.
Henry Billy, I'm little Henry.
Billy (*laughing*) Don't be daft, tha's not little Henry. (*Frightened*) Tha's a stranger. I'm not allowed to speak to thee.

Billy exits

Henry bursts into tears

Hilda (*with great effort*) Being a spinster, I know nowt about it. I've never fooled mesen. But I wanted to tell tha Ezra were never the same man after the Good Lord took Ada from us wi' that bus. (*She sniffs*) Ee, our Doris! I was wrong to want thee all to mesen. We'll both be strangers to thee in t'long run, no matter what.

Hilda exits

Doris If I'd had a son of my own, which I haven't, business always came first, and those journeys to Cap Ferrat really took it out of me, but if I had a son I'd want him to look just like you. I wouldn't mind a bit.

Aunty Doris begins to exit, realizes her error, decides she can do nothing about it and continues out

Lorna Arrow enters

Henry Lorna Arrow!
Lorna I were broken-hearted when tha threw me over. I cried for months.
Henry Gerraway!

Pause

I wouldn't throw you over now.
Lorna (*knowing the answer*) Why?
Henry You've become a real beauty.
Lorna You haven't.
Henry I'm still waiting to grow out of podgy stage.
Lorna Tha's still my Henry, though. Does tha remember t'barn where tha used to read t'comics to me?

Lorna Arrow exits

Henry Oh ay. It's still there, is it?
Doris (*calling off*) Time, gentlemen please!
Henry (*calling off*) I'm just going out for a breath of air.

Henry exits

Geoffrey (*off*) Don't do anything I wouldn't do.
Doris (*off*) Geoffrey, really! Henry was being discreet.
Geoffrey (*off*) Doris!

An owl hoots. A starlit sky

  Henry and Lorna enter

Henry This barn hasn't changed much.
Lorna We should have brought us comics wi' us.
Henry I don't want to read tonight.
Lorna There's better things to do.
Henry Oh, Lorna, I'm going away tomorrow. National Service.
Lorna Oh, Henry.
Henry It's my last night.
Lorna Which would tha prefer, Henry, sixteen thousand tons of sweet coupons, or me taking all me clothes off?

Music. "The Dambusters' March", it continues under the next scene

SCENE 30

The Lights come up on Henry meeting a Sergeant-Major

Sergeant-Major Oy, you, what are you doing?
Henry Sorry, were you talking to me? I didn't hear you. I was thinking.
Sergeant-Major You were what! You was thinking? You're in the army now! What's your name?
Henry (*to himself*) Oh no, here we go again. (*To him*) Pratt, sir.
Sergeant-Major Pratt! You know what you are, Pratt? You're a short, fat, gob of rancid goat droppings.
Henry (*quietly triumphant*) Yes, sir. If you say so, sir.

"The Dambusters' March" swells up. Slide sequence

End of play

FURNITURE AND PROPERTY LIST

SCENE 1

On stage: Chairs
Table
Newspaper for **Ezra**
Cloth by **Parrot**

SCENE 2

On stage: As Scene 1

SCENE 3

On stage: Nil
Off stage: Picnic basket **(Ezra)**

SCENE 4

On stage: As Scene 1

SCENE 5

On stage: As Scene 1

SCENE 6

On stage: Nil

SCENE 7

On stage: Comic for **Henry**
Off stage: Hoe **(Eric)**

SCENE 8

On stage: Train seats

SCENE 9

On stage: Desk
Chair

SCENE 10

On stage: Desks
Chairs

SCENE 11

On stage: As Scene 1
Set: Pencil, exercise book, *Biggles* book on table

SCENE 12

On stage: Table. *On it:* empty plate and cutlery
Chairs

SCENE 13

On stage: Desk
Chairs

Off stage: Briefcase containing essay (**Mr Quell**)

SCENE 14

On stage: As Scene 1

Off stage: Briefcase (**Mr Quell**)
Lighted torch (**Teddy**)

SCENE 15

On stage: Settee
Chairs
Table. *On it:* drinks

SCENE 16

On stage: As Scene 15

Strike: Drinks

Set: Suitcase with clothes
Drink for **Doris**

Personal: **Hilda:** letter
Doris: handkerchief

SCENE 17

On stage: Tram seats
Bag for **Henry**

SCENE 18

On stage: As Scene 15

SCENE 19

On stage: Chairs
Table. *On it:* drinks
Small stage. *On it:* magic tricks

SCENE 20

On stage: Nil

SCENE 21

On stage: Nil

Off stage: Cricket bat (**Tosser**)

Personal: **Tosser:** money

SCENE 22

On stage: Chair
Desk

SCENE 23

On stage: Picnic basket with food, flask of tea, etc.

SCENE 24

On stage: Small stage
Mortar board, gown, comic false nose and moustache for **Henry**
Sheet for **Lampo**

SCENE 25

On stage: Nil

Personal: **Doris:** handbag

SCENE 26

On stage: Table. *On it:* *Biggles* book wrapped in brown paper
Chairs

SCENE 27

On stage: Tram seats
Bible for **Mabel**

SCENE 28

On stage: Nil

Off stage: Rucksack **(Mabel)**

SCENE 29

On stage: Table. *On it:* drink, newspaper
Chairs

Off stage: Coins **(Billy)**

SCENE 30

On stage: Nil

LIGHTING PLOT

Property fittings required: nil

Various simple interior and exterior settings

Scene 1

To open: General interior lighting

Cue 1	**Ezra** exits *Fade lighting slightly*	(Page 3)
Cue 2	**Parrot** finally dies *Fade lighting*	(Page 4)

Scene 2

To open: General interior lighting

Cue 3	**Ada:** "... make it up to him, now." *Fade lighting*	(Page 5)

Scene 3

To open: Exterior lighting

Cue 4	**Ezra:** "Oh heck." *Fade lighting*	(Page 5)

Scene 4

To open: Interior lighting

Cue 5	**Ada:** "I'll just make t'door." *Fade lighting slightly*	(Page 7)

Scene 5

To open: Interior lighting

Cue 6	**Teddy:** "I'm the one who's sick." *Fade lighting*	(Page 9)

Scene 6

To open: Exterior lighting

Cue 7	**Henry:** "... and work wi' you on t'farm." *Fade lighting*	(Page 10)

Scene 7

To open: Barn lighting

Cue 8   **Lorna** exits, screaming tearfully   (Page 12)
           Fade lighting

Scene 8

To open: Train lighting

Cue 9   **Henry:** "Oh double heck."   (Page 13)
           Fade lighting

Scene 9

To open: Interior lighting on study

Cue 10   **Miss Forest:** ". . . the catering to you?"   (Page 14)
           Fade lighting

Scene 10

To open: Classroom lighting

Cue 11   **Henry:** "Oh ay, Miss."   (Page 15)
           Change to playground lighting

Cue 12   **Gang:** "Bye, Henry."   (Page 16)
           Fade lighting

Scene 11

To open: Interior lighting on Henry's house

Cue 13   **Cousin Hilda** exits   (Page 18)
           Fade lighting

Scene 12

To open: Interior lighting on Hilda's house

Cue 14   **Henry** rushes about playing aeroplanes   (Page 20)
           Fade lighting

Scene 13

To open: Interior lighting on school

Cue 15   **Mr Quell:** ". . . where they live?"   (Page 21)
           Fade lighting

Scene 14

To open: Interior lighting on Henry's house

Cue 16   **Hilda:** ". . . wasting batteries."   (Page 23)
           Fade lighting

INTERVAL

SCENE 15

To open: General lighting on Aunty Doris's and Uncle Teddy's house

Cue 17   **Daphne:** "Love you." Doris glares   (Page 25)
          Fade lighting

SCENE 16

To open: Interior lighting on Aunty Doris's house

Cue 18   **Doris** stares at **Teddy** in horror   (Page 27)
          Fade lighting

SCENE 17

To open: Lighting on tram

Cue 19   **Henry** starts his picnic   (Page 28)
          Fade lighting

SCENE 18

To open: Interior lighting on Aunty Doris's house

Cue 20   **Henry:** "... into your life!"   (Page 29)
          Fade lighting

SCENE 19

To open: Interior lighting on club

Cue 21   **Uncle Teddy** and **Aunty Doris** sink, their heads in their hands   (Page 31)
          Fade lighting

SCENE 20

To open: Lighting on college

Cue 22   **Paul** and **Henry** look at each other   (Page 32)
          Fade lighting

SCENE 21

To open: Exterior lighting on cricket field

Cue 23   **Henry** stands looking at the money in his hand   (Page 33)
          Fade lighting

SCENE 22

To open: Interior lighting on Lampo's study

Cue 24   **Lampo:** "... does have its drawbacks."   (Page 35)
          Fade lighting

SCENE 23

To open: Exterior lighting on picnic

Cue 25   **Mrs Hargreaves:** "... his knowledge of people."   (Page 36)
             Fade lighting

SCENE 24

To open: Lighting on wings and school stage

Cue 26   As music swells (*There'll Always be an England*)   (Page 37)
             Fade lighting

SCENE 25

To open: Lighting on **Henry** and **Aunty Doris**

Cue 27   **Doris:** "... with Cousin Hilda, of course."   (Page 38)
             Fade lighting

SCENE 26

To open: Interior lighting on **Hilda**'s house

Cue 28   **Hilda:** "... tha likes brawn."   (Page 39)
             Fade lighting

SCENE 27

To open: Lighting on tram

Cue 29   **Conductor:** "Heaven help thy mother."   (Page 39)
             Fade lighting

SCENE 28

To open: Exterior lighting

Cue 30   **Mr Quell:** "... in the Yorkshire Ganges."   (Page 41)
             Fade lighting

SCENE 29

To open: Pub lighting

Cue 31   **Geoffrey** (off): "Doris!"   (Page 45)
             Cross-fade to exterior lighting and a starlit sky

Cue 32   **Lorna:** "... all me clothes off?"   (Page 46)
             Fade lighting

SCENE 30

To open: General lighting

No cues

EFFECTS PLOT

SCENES 1–14

Cue 1 As Scene 1 opens   (Page 1)
  Busker performs, train rushes over viaduct, tram rattles by, clock ticks

Cue 2 **Ezra:** "... today of all days?"   (Page 1)
  Pause, then clock ticks

Cue 3 **Cousin Hilda** exits   (Page 2)
  Clock ticks

Cue 4 **Parrot:** "Bugger off!"   (Page 3)
  Music, noise of Ezra, Ada, Hilda and Norah sleeping

Cue 5 **Parrot** dies finally   (Page 4)
  Music: "There'll Always Be An England"

Cue 6 **Ada:** "... make it up to him now."   (Page 5)
  Music

Cue 7 As Scene 3 opens   (Page 5)
  Tram ride, bus ride, sounds of town merging into country

Cue 8 **Ezra:** "Oh heck."   (Page 5)
  Radio comedy programme—fade as Scene 4 begins

Cue 9 **Ada:** "I'll just make t'door."   (Page 7)
  Music, then sound of ancient bed-springs

Cue 10 **Ada:** "Gerraway wi' yer. Oh. Ah."   (Page 7)
  Bed-springs

Cue 11 **Ezra:** "... our Henry, hell's bells!"   (Page 7)
  Music

Cue 12 **Teddy:** "... I'm the one who's sick."   (Page 9)
  Music

Cue 13 As Scene 6 opens   (Page 9)
  Winter countryside sounds, sheep to the fore

Cue 14 **Henry:** "... work wi' you on t'farm."   (Page 10)
  Music

Cue 15 **Lorna** exits tearfully   (Page 12)
  Music

Cue 16 As Scene 8 opens   (Page 12)
  Sounds of third division football match, then train journey

Cue 17 **Henry:** "Oh double heck."   (Page 13)
  Music

Cue 38   **Compère** (*off*): "... the Tadcaster Thrush."   (Page 30)
          Sporadic applause

Cue 39   **Tadcaster Thrush** exits   (Page 31)
          Dribble of applause

Cue 40   **Uncle Teddy** and **Aunty Doris** sink, their heads in their hands   (Page 31)
          Music

Cue 41   **Paul** and **Henry** look at each other   (Page 32)
          Music

Cue 42   As Scene 21 opens   (Page 32)
          Sounds of birds and cricket match

Cue 43   **Henry** laughs, **Lampo** doesn't   (Page 32)
          Applause, off

Cue 44   **Henry:** "... compared with Tuscany."   (Page 33)
          Applause, off

Cue 45   **Lampo** exits   (Page 33)
          Applause and cheers, off

Cue 46   **Henry** stands looking at the money in his hand   (Page 33)
          Music

Cue 47   **Lampo:** "... does have its drawbacks."   (Page 35)
          Music

Cue 48   **Mrs Hargreaves:** "... his knowledge of people."   (Page 36)
          Music

Cue 49   As **Lampo** goes on school stage to do his turn   (Page 36)
          Music: the "Baccarole" from "Orpheus in the Underworld"

Cue 50   **Lampo** finishes his turn   (Page 36)
          Slight applause

Cue 51   **Henry** comes on to school stage   (Page 36)
          Warm applause

Cue 52   As **Henry**'s act comes to an end   (Page 37)
          Applause, music swells up: "There'll Always Be An England

Cue 53   **Doris:** "... with Cousin Hilda, of course."   (Page 38)
          Music

Cue 54   **Hilda:** "... tha likes brawn."   (Page 39)
          Music

Cue 55   When ready for Scene 27   (Page 39)
          Tram sounds

Cue 56   **Conductor:** "... heaven help thy mother."   (Page 39)
          Large splash and slurping sound, off; music

Cue 57   As Scene 28 opens   (Page 40)
          Country sounds

Cue 58   **Mabel Billington** exits   (Page 41)
          Loud siren

Cue 59	**Mr Quell:** "... in the Yorkshire Ganges." *Loud siren; music*	(Page 41)
Cue 60	As Scene 29 opens *Pub noises*	(Page 42)
Cue 61	**Geoffrey** (*off*): "Doris!" *Fade pub noises; owl hoots*	(Page 45)
Cue 62	**Lorna:** "... all me clothes off?" *Music: "The Dambusters' March"—continue under next scene*	(Page 46)
Cue 63	**Henry:** "If you say so, sir." *Music swells up*	(Page 46)

SLIDE PLOT

Slides: newspaper headlines and photographs

Cue 1	Pre-show Smoky, northern industrial landscape of roof-tops and chimneys framed in leaves—suggesting Henry's birthplace	(Page 1)
Cue 2	Before Scene 1 Another panorama of a northern town A busker performing to a cinema queue, or a cinema A train A tram Roofs of back to backs Interior of a back to back, close up of a clock on a mantelpiece	(Page 1)
Cue 3	Middle of Scene 1, **Ezra** exits Interior of a back to back, bedroom	(Page 3)
Cue 4	After Scene 1 Interior again A headline for Friday March 13th, 1935 The *Daily Mirror* of Monday, March 18th, 1935. The headlines include "German Arms—Cabinet Acts" and "Will Sir John Simon Go to Berlin"	(Page 4)

A photo of Hitler with a party of officials
The *Sheffield Telegraph* of March 18th, 1935. "Hitler Conscription Bombshell" and "Shock to British Ministers"
Sheffield Telegraph, Friday July 24th, 1936. "Arrival of the Olympic Torch". Photo of torch arriving flanked by Nazis
"Black Flash, Jessie Owens of USA Wins Olympic Heat by Yards". Photos of Jessie Owens, and of Hitler watching a Nazi javelin thrower
Sheffield Telegraph, Monday, October 5th, 1936. "Fascist March Banned After Ugly Scenes. Baton Charges, Many Arrests"
Sheffield Telegraph, Saturday, October 17th, 1936. "Jarrow Marchers Arrive in Sheffield". Photo of marchers with banner
Sheffield Telegraph of Friday, December 11th, 1936. "Abdication of Edward VIII. Duke of York to Succeed to the Throne"
Daily Express, Thursday, September 15th, 1938. "Premier is Flying to See Hitler"
Photo of coloured man and white worker together
Photo of Hitler and Chamberlain together
Cartoon of clouds over Europe, with ominous black figures of industrial aristocrats, and a band of Jarrow Marchers in the centre

Cue 5   After Scene 2   (Page 5)
Photos of Len Hutton in mid-stroke and Len Hutton raising his cap to acknowledge applause

Cue 6   After Scene 3   (Page 5)
"No War For Britain, Premier Brings Back Four Point Peace Proposal". Photo of Chamberlain reading a letter from the King. "Multitude Cheer the Premier Home and Hear Him Say, 'You May Sleep Quietly, It Is Peace In Our Time.'"
Chamberlain at a microphone, giving a public address
A man and a woman, (**Ezra** and **Ada**), at the breakfast table, listening to the news on the wireless
"I Cannot Abandon My Peace Efforts, Premier Issues Dramatic 1.00 a.m. Statement". "Incredible That Europe Should Be Plunged Into Bloody Struggle". "London Digs Trenches At Night"
Sheffield Telegraph and Independent, Friday September 1st, 1939. "Sensational German Moves Today", "Polish Towns Bombed", "General Fighting." "Hitler Proclaims We Meet Force with Force"
Sheffield Telegraph and Independent, Saturday September 2nd, 1939. "Sheffield Evacuees Arrive". Photo of hordes of children arriving in the town
Neville Chamberlain at a studio microphone

Cue 7   Middle of Scene 4—**Ada:** "I'll just make t'door."   (Page 7)
Photo of two parrots kissing

Cue 8   After Scene 4   (Page 7)
Three scruffy little toddlers on the bridge over the Rundle Canal, peering through a fence
Arthur Askey and Richard Murdoch at a radio microphone

A group of ARP wardens in their office (**Ezra** in the centre)
A man (**Ezra**), in uniform, kissing a woman (**Ada**), goodbye on
the doorstep
Sheffield Telegraph and Independent, Tuesday, September 5th,
1939. "British Planes in Action", "RAF Bomb German Fleet"
Two women who could be **Ada** and **Her Mother**, go out
shopping, dressed in black and looking mournful

Cue 9   After Scene 5   (Page 9)
A woman who might be **Aunty Doris**, posing by their expensive
new car.
Portrait of distraught **Ada** and **Henry** types crying as they leave
to go to Low Farm
A poster showing a child wandering in the rubble of a bombed
building. A slogan on the wall says, "Your Britain, Fight For It
Now"
Poster with two panels. The left-hand panel shows a man in a
crowd speaking, and the slogan, "Freedom of Speech", the
right-hand panel shows people praying, with the slogan, "Free-
dom of Worship"
Poster with two panels. The left-hand panel shows a family
round a large roast dinner with the slogan, "Freedom from
Want". The right-hand panel show parents tucking children
into bed, with the slogan, "Freedom from Fear"
Picture News showing, "England Speeds Up", and "Gas Mask
Rush Goes On—Trenches Are Dug, Sandbag Defence Work
Begins"
The *Sheffield Telegraph and Independent*, Saturday December
14th, 1940. "Widespread Havoc After Furious Nazi Blitz on
Sheffield"
A farm landscape, which could be "Low Farm". Three dray
horses pull a reaping machine across a cornfield

Cue 10   After Scene 6   (Page 10)
The *Daily Express*, Friday May 10th, 1940. "Churchill
Expected to Be New Premier", "Chamberlain to Resign", and
"Socialists Refuse to Join New Cabinet, But They May Back
Winston"
Ration Day, 1940, "Lump for a Pal Barter in Cafés. Silk
Stockings and Suits May Need Coupons"
Sheffield Telegraph and Independent, Wednesday, June 5th
1940, "RAF Fights Narrow Corridor to Dunkirk"
A group of five-year-olds sit in desks at a village school, which
could be Rowth Bridge. A boy who could be **Henry** sits in the
front row
Two people pick their way through the blitzed wreckage of a
street in Sheffield

Cue 11   After Scene 7   (Page 12)
A football crowd on the terraces
Interior of a train

Cue 12   After Scene 8   (Page 13)
Sheffield Telegraph and Independent, Tuesday, August 27th,
1940. "German Attacks Broken—46 Down", "London Had

Longest Raid Yet", "Bombs on Outskirts During Night"
Newspaper cartoon, of a theatre with captions, "Blitz—Victory
Opera House", "Downfall of Britain—Someday"
Two burnt-out trams surrounded by blitzed buildings in Shef-
field
Sheffield Telegraph and Independent, Monday December 8th,
1941. "Japan Declares War on Britain and United States", "US
Bases Raided. Battleships Set on Fire", "British Gunboat
Sunk", "Parliament Meets Today as US Army is Mobilized"
Sheffield Telegraph and Independent, Friday December 12th,
1941, "US Declare War on Germany and Italy". "Moscow
Children are Evacuated. Sent South with Their Mothers"
Sheffield Telegraph, Monday February 1st, 1941, "Stalingrad
Army Wiped Out", "Fifteen Generals Taken, 330,000 Liqui-
dated"
Sheffield Telegraph, Thursday, November 5th, 1942. "Rommel
is in Full Retreat", "Disordered Columns Bombed and Chased
Night and Day"
Sheffield Telegraph, Thursday September 9th, 1943, "Allies
Land at Many Points After Surrender of Italy"
Sheffield Telegraph, "Education Bill Gets Second Reading
Without Divisions", "Labour Hails Long Overdue Reforms"
Daily Express, Saturday August 26th, 1944, "Paris is Freed.
Germans Surrender to French"
Sheffield Telegraph, Thursday February 15th, 1945, "7000
Planes Batter Reich from East to West. Blazing Dresden
Beacon for Soviets"
Sheffield Telegraph, Wednesday May 2nd, 1945, "Hitler is
Dead. Doenitz is Leader of Germany"
Photo of VE Day celebrations, at a school which could be
Henry's

Cue 13   After Scene 9   (Page 14)
         The Crazy Gang at a BBC microphone
         Photo of a school classroom

Cue 14   Middle of Scene 10   (Page 15)
         Photo of a school playground

Cue 15   After Scene 10   (Page 16)
         Photo of terraced streets. A pub which could be **Ezra**'s local. A
         group of men drinking outside

Cue 16   After Scene 11   (Page 18)
         Article from *Picture Post*, by Thomas Balough, "The First
         Necessity in the New Britain is Work for All"
         Article from *Picture Post*, "A New Britain Must Be Planned"

Cue 17   After Scene 12   (Page 20)
         Sheffield Telegraph, Thursday August 7th, 1945, "Atom
         Bomb—Churchill Warns of Terrible Means", "Allies Have
         Won Biggest Gamble in History", "Smoke and Dust Hide
         Hiroshima"
         Daily Express, Wednesday, August 8th, 1945, "How We
         Dropped It by Atomic Raiders", "Bomb Shook Us 10 Miles
         Away"

Sheffield Telegraph, Friday August 10th, 1945. "Truman Gives Japan the Final Choice", "Surrender or Atom Bomb Will Slay Thousands"
Sheffield Telegraph, Wednesday, August 15th, 1945, "World War Ends—Total Japanese Surrender", "MacArthur Will Receive Enemy Envoys", "Today and Tomorrow Public Holidays"

Cue 18   After Scene 13   (Page 21)
A man who could be **Ezra**, and other men plus two bedraggled dogs in another of **Ezra**'s local pubs

Cue 19   After Scene 14   (Page 23)
A woman who could be **Aunty Doris** is standing by her expensive car
Terraced northern street, washing, a man like **Ezra** wearing a flat cap, and carrying a newspaper, walking
Smoky, northern industrial landscape, as cue 1, for interval

Cue 20   Before Scene 15   (Page 24)
Sheffield Telegraph, Friday March 12th, 1946, "Margarine and Soap May Be Cut Next, but US Will Be Shipping Dried Eggs", "Storm Rising Over Health Bill"
Sheffield Telegraph, Friday June 6th, 1947, "Marshall to Europe", "Unite for More Aid", "US Will Oppose Any Bid to Block Recovery"
Photo of an **Aunty Doris** type interior

Cue 21   After Scene 15   (Page 25)
Daily Express, November 21st, 1947. Photo of Prince Phillip and Princess Elizabeth on their wedding day. "Royal Family Join Crowd", "A Wonderful Day Says the Queen"
Sheffield Telegraph, Friday November 21st, 1947, "*Honeymoon Town Acclaims Royal Pair*", "*We've Had a Wonderful Day—The Princess*"
Photo of a group of public schoolboys in top hats and tails buying flowers from a street flower-seller
Photo of hunt assembling in front of a stately home
Photo of seven Oxbridge undergraduates

Cue 22   After Scene 16   (Page 27)
October 23rd, 1947, "Reagan Warns Against Witch-hunt", Macarthyism
November 13th, 1947, "Chancellor Resigns Over Budget Leak"
January 30th, 1947, "Ghandi Assassinated"
Photo of interior of a tram

Cue 23   After Scene 17   (Page 28)
Photo of Paradise Lane
Photo of a couple, reference to **Aunty Doris** and **Geoffrey Porringer**

Cue 24   After Scene 18   (Page 29)
Photo refering to working men's clubs, or cabarets

Cue 25   After Scene 19   (Page 31)
Newspaper advertisement, "Why Rupture Sufferers Dread the

Winter"
Public school photo

Cue 26   After Scene 20   (Page 32)
            May 14th, 1948, "Israel is Born"
            July 5th 1948, "NHS Begins Care from Cradle to the Grave"
            March 18th 1949, "Plans for NATO Unveiled"
            May 12th, 1949, "End of Berlin Blockade"
            May 23rd, 1949, "Western Sector of Divided Germany is a
            Federal Republic"
            Another public school photo

Cue 27   After Scene 21   (Page 33)
            Public school photo

Cue 28   After Scene 22   (Page 35)
            Biggles reference, photo of heroic airmen
            Photo of a woman like Mrs Hargreaves, beautiful and elegant,
            with a fur wrap
            "Debutantes Scurry from Rain at Royal Garden Party"
            Photo of debutantes
            Photo of a Glyndebourne-type picnic

Cue 29   After Scene 23   (Page 36)
            Photo of two little boys, in a yard surrounded by brick walls;
            they are urinating in a puddle
            Sheffield Telegraph, "The Real Cripps is Warm, Human,
            Friendly"
            Photo of Sir Stafford Cripps

Cue 30   After Scene 24   (Page 37)
            Photo, back view of a man we assume to be **Ezra**, alone except
            for a little mongrel dog

Cue 31   After Scene 25   (Page 38)
            Propaganda advertisement, cartoon of a dolly sewing, "Make
            Do and Mend, Says Mrs Sew And Sew"
            Photo of a street with telegraph poles, hoardings and in the far
            distance semi-detached houses. The grim environment of **Cou-
            sin Hilda**'s home

Cue 32   After Scene 26   (Page 39)
            Photo of a tram

Cue 33   After Scene 27   (Page 39)
            July, 1950, "Korean Conflict Begins to Suck in World Powers"
            Sheffield Telegraph, Saturday November 25th, 1950, "Election
            in Two Months?", "Labour's Majority Cannot Be More Than
            16", "Socialists Will Try to Carry on Without Liberals' Help"
            May 15th, 1951, "Lavish Festival Gives Britain a Pat on the
            Back"
            Photo of Yorkshire countryside and coal mines

Cue 34   After Scene 28   (Page 41)
            Photo of coal mines
            Photo of the Coronation
            Photos of **Henry** as a young boy

Cue 35   After Scene 30   (Page 46)
A peaceful farm which could be Low Farm. A drawing of an English rustic scene with a church in the background. In the foreground, a field in which a family are resting by their tractor during harvest
Propaganda poster, "Your Britain, Fight For It Now". A rustic scene with a shepherd walking behind his flock in autumnal fields
A family which could be the **Pratts**, gathered round in their home. A man, **Ezra**, in shirt-sleeves, a woman, **Ada**, bathing a naked baby in an enamel bowl in front of a coal fire
A gang, the Paradise Lane gang, about to fire a catapult
Sheffield Telegraph, Tuesday September 26th, 1944, "National Insurance Plan", "Government Aims to Banish Want, Misery, Inefficiency", "Benefits Designed to Raise Family Life Standards"
Undergraduate election posters showing a group of well-heeled undergraduates
Daily Mirror, Friday March 13th, the day of **Henry**'s birth, "Golden Miller Wins Fourth Gold Cup at Cheltenham"
An industrial landscape viewed across a foreground of fields, "a mucky picture set in a golden frame" as **Ezra** says
A woman who could be **Ada**, hanging out washing across terraced back to back houses—Paradise Lane
Sheffield Telegraph, "Third Century in Successive Matches. Len Hutton is a Truly Great Yorkshireman"

MADE AND PRINTED IN GREAT BRITAIN BY
LATIMER TREND & COMPANY LTD PLYMOUTH

MADE IN ENGLAND

Printed in May 2023
by Rotomail Italia S.p.A., Vignate (MI) - Italy

Second from Last in
the Sack Race

A Play

Michael Birch

A Samuel French Acting Edition

SAMUEL
FRENCH
FOUNDED 1830

SAMUELFRENCH-LONDON.CO.UK
SAMUELFRENCH.COM

ISBN 978-0-573-01900-5

www.samuelfrench-london.co.uk

www.samuelfrench.com

FOR AMATEUR PRODUCTION ENQUIRIES

UNITED KINGDOM AND WORLD
EXCLUDING NORTH AMERICA

plays@SamuelFrench-London.co.uk

020 7255 4302/01

Each title is subject to availability from Samuel French,

depending upon country of performance.

SECOND FROM LAST IN THE SACK RACE

Second from Last in the Sack Race was performed at the West Yorkshire Playhouse in November 1990 with the following cast:

Susie Baxter
Abi Rayment
Paul Slack
James Warrior
John Webb

Director   Jude Kelly
Designer   Sally Crabbe

The play takes place in the north and south of England
Time 1935–1953

CHARACTERS

Ezra Pratt, Henry's put-upon father
A Parrot, Henry's mother's surprising parrot
A Radio, Henry's household wireless
Cousin Hilda, Henry's grown-up severe second cousin
Norah, Henry's pessimistic maternal grandmother
Henry Pratt
Ada Pratt, Henry's mother, Norah's stoic daughter
Aunty Doris, Henry's aunty, Ada's snobby sister
Uncle Teddy, Henry's uncle, Doris's shifty husband
Billy, The Half-Wit, Henry's country friend
Eric Lugg, Henry's foe with the hoe
Lorna Arrow, Henry's forward first girlfriend
Miss Candy, Henry's dedicated first teacher
Miss Forest, Henry's desiccated headmistress
Mr Gibbins, Henry's weary second teacher
Tommy Marsden, Henry's gang's intimidating leader
Martin Hammond ⎫
Basher ⎬ gang members
Slasher ⎭
Liam O'Reilly, Henry's Cousin Hilda's confidante
Mr Quell, Henry's perceptive third teacher
Geoffrey Porringer, Henry's aunty's lover with black-heads
Daphne Porringer, Henry's aunty's lover's wife without
Mabel Billington, Henry's religious girlfriend
A Tram Conductor, Henry's tram conductor at crucial times
A Club Compère, Henry's first cabaret announcer
The Amazing Illingworth, Henry's first magic act
The Tadcaster Thrush, Henry's first cabaret singer
Paul Hargreaves, Henry's posh public school friend
Mr Hargreaves ⎫
Mrs Hargreaves ⎬ Henry's posh public school friend's
Diana Hargreaves ⎭ family
Tosser Pilkington-Brick, Henry's top-drawer sports hero
Lampo Davey, Henry's upper-class artistic mentor
The Sergeant-Major, Henry's first Sergeant-Major